The Ch
Love

A Victorian family history

An account of the seven
children of
John Llewelyn Davies & Mary Crompton

by

Jane Wynne Willson

Garland Publications

Published by Garland Publications

December 2007

Printed in the USA by Lulu

This book is currently available in the UK from:

Garland Publications, 28 Garland Way

Northfield, Birmingham B31 2BT

www.garlandpublications.co.uk

Front cover designed by William Wynne Willson from the oil portrait of
Mary Llewelyn Davies by Sir William Blake Richmond

Contents

The Llewelyn Davies family

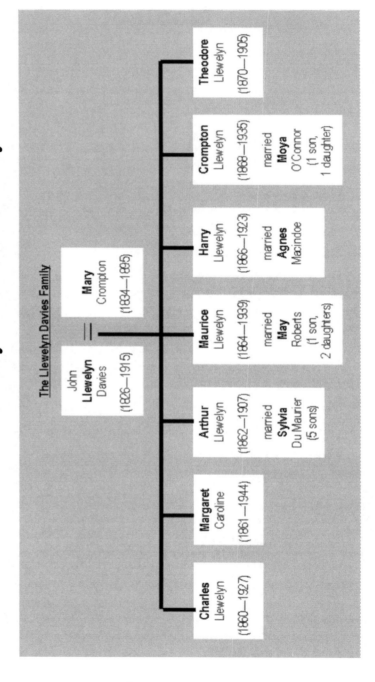

The Llewelyn Davies Family

John **Llewelyn** Davies (1826—1915) = **Mary** Crompton (1834—1895)

Charles Llewelyn (1860—1927)

Margaret Caroline (1861—1944)

Arthur Llewelyn (1862—1907)
married **Sylvia** Du Maurier (5 sons)

Maurice Llewelyn (1864—1939)
married **May** Roberts (1 son, 2 daughters)

Harry Llewelyn (1866—1923)
married **Agnes** Mazindoe

Crompton Llewelyn (1868—1935)
married **Moya** O'Connor (1 son, 1 daughter)

Theodore Llewelyn (1870—1905)

Preface

On June 29th 1860 Charles Llewelyn Davies was born at no.18, Blandford Square in the London borough of Marylebone. He was the first child of the Rev. John Llewelyn Davies, then Rector of Christ Church, Marylebone, and his wife, Mary Crompton.

In the ten years that followed the birth of Charley (as he was generally known), six more children were born: Margaret Caroline in 1861, Arthur Llewelyn in 1863, Maurice Llewelyn in 1864, Harry Llewelyn in 1866, Crompton Llewelyn in 1868 and Theodore Llewelyn in 1870.

A family of seven children was not particularly unusual in those days. More unusual were the family members themselves, both as individuals and in their relationship with each other. They were described by their maternal uncle Charles Crompton as 'that happiest of families'; Peter Llewelyn Davies, Arthur's third son, wrote 'they were all equally affectionate to each other – a most united family'; while their mother, Mary Crompton, referred to her seven children as 'the chain of love.' This last description has given me the title for this book in which I am attempting to build up an impression of the kind of people they were, gleaned from an assortment of family papers and letters, from archive material and, in some instances, from stories passed down by word of mouth and from my own memory. I am one of the granddaughters of Maurice Llewelyn Davies, the fourth child in the family.

In order to put the Llewelyn Davies family in some sort of context, I will give a brief outline of their Davies and Crompton forebears, based on what material I have managed to unearth. On the Davies side much of this comes from a *Chronicle*, written in old age by their aunt, Emily Davies, best known as the founder of Girton College, the first college for women in Cambridge. This *Chronicle*, and other Llewelyn Davies family papers, were collected and annotated by Emily's great nephew, Peter Llewelyn Davies, the publisher, in the 1940s in what he entitled '*The Morgue*'. This was never published but much of it is now available on the Internet.

My information on the Cromptons is more patchy, although the Crompton relations seem to have had the greater influence on the lives of the Llewelyn Davies children as they grew up.

An assortment of further material which seems to me of interest is attached in two appendices.

Jane Wynne Willson, Birmingham 2007

The Rev. John and Mary Davies and family

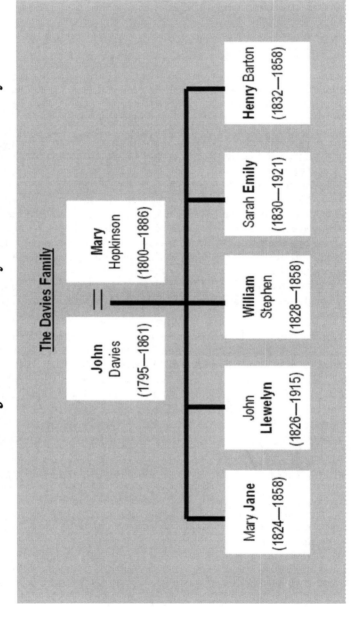

The Davies Family

| John Davies (1795—1861) | = | Mary Hopkinson (1800—1886) |

- Mary Jane (1824—1858)
- John Llewelyn (1826—1915)
- William Stephen (1828—1858)
- Sarah Emily (1830—1921)
- Henry Barton (1832—1858)

1 The Davies Family

John Llewelyn Davies was the eldest son of the Rev. John Davies, a leading evangelical churchman and academic. The Rev. John Davies was born at Llandewi Brefi in Cardiganshire in 1795. His father was James Davies, who farmed land at Hendre Philip and liked to claim descent from Llewelyn ap Gruffydd, the ill-fated and last Prince of Wales. Unfortunately there is no firm evidence for this and a small bit of research suggests that the Prince died without legitimate issue.

One account of the family states that James the farmer, on the death of his wife Jane Richards, emigrated to America, leaving his only son John to be brought up by a maternal uncle. Emily Davies, however, John Llewelyn Davies's sister, in her *Chronicle*, states that her father John was one of five children. She further recounts how, at a later date, John helped his younger brother Stephen go to Cambridge. It seems likely that James took his other children to America with him at the time of his wife's death but left John with his uncle, since he was happily settled at school at Lampeter College. There he was known as 'Horace Bach' (or little Horace) because of his proficiency in Latin. John was extremely bright. At 13 he was a tutor 'in a gentleman's family' and at 14 an 'usher' (or teacher) in a school.

It is known that he studied at Oxford for a short time and then moved to Queen's College, Cambridge before being ordained. His first ecclesiastical post was at Chichester and there he met and married Mary Hopkinson from Derby, who was a few years younger than himself. Her father was described by Emily Davies in her *Chronicle* as being 'in business as a manufacturer of fuller's earth'. The Hopkinson grandparents were evidently quite wealthy. According to Emily, they lived frugally and only kept one servant. She wrote:

> 'I once asked my mother what they did with their money. Her reply was: "They saved it, for us."'

John and Mary Davies started a boarding school for boys and, after the birth of their first two children Mary Jane (in 1824) and John Llewelyn (in 1826), moved together with the school to Southampton. Here the next two children were born, William Stephen (in 1828) and Sarah Emily (in 1830).

It was during the period at Southampton that John Davies, as well as teaching at the school, was writing his magnum opus, '*An Estimate of the Human Mind: a Philosophical Inquiry into the Legitimate Application and Extent of its Leading Faculties, as connected with the Principles and Obligations of the Christian Religion*'. This is an immensely learned and, one might say, obscure book and the enlarged, second edition [of which I have a copy] runs to 630 pages. I can well understand why, according to his daughter's account:

'this involved long hours of work, and he used to speak of how he tied a wet towel round his head to keep himself awake.'

This was one of twenty publications, and the one for which he became best known.

The Davies's fifth and last child, Henry Barton, was born in 1832 and, soon after, Mary Davies first mentions in her diary that 'my beloved husband's health began to fail.' Over the next years the family made several moves in the hope of helping John Davies's health including, in 1833, a year's stay at Avranches in France. Llewelyn , as he was always called in the family in preference to John, was sent to board at a school (which he calls 'College') nearby.

He wrote the following letter to his father at the age of seven, away at school over Christmas which seems a bit sad, though he sounds cheerful enough. I am including it as it shows, as well as a rather remarkable command of English, an easy relationship with his father. The spelling and grammar mistakes are as in the original:

Llewelyn aged 7

December 31st 1833

My dear Papa,

I hope you are quite well. I hope Mamma is quite well. I hope that I get on at College. Monsieur Pignois says I do my devoir's very well and I hope I shall get the top of my class the next time. I am glad you came here because I like to go to College very much. I see the shops full of glass boxes, and in the confectioners there are toys and sugar men and dogs and cats and soldiers and all sorts of things. The toy shops are full of play guns and wooden swords etc. My nitted socks fit me quite well and I like them very much.

On Christmas-day we had church and they all took sacraments and gave money. We got 21 francs. I have got a penknife and it got a little point at the end of it to split the pens. It cost 15 frs. And it was for a new year's present because I wanted it so much. My knife was bought at Madame Roffare.

I'm your affectionate son,

J.L.Davies.

In 1840 John Davies was appointed Rector of Gateshead. His health seems to have improved at this time and he remained in this position for 21 years, until his death in 1861 at the age of 66. While at Gateshead the three boys attended a small foundation school daily, while Jane and Emily had lessons in French, Italian and music at home. Emily wrote: 'Our education answered to the description of that of clergymen's daughters generally.'

In 1842, at the age of 16, Llewelyn was sent to Repton and, from there, went to Trinity College, Cambridge where he had a distinguished academic career, was President of the Union and was made a fellow in 1850. William, who was said to have been equally clever, followed him to Repton and Cambridge but evidently, for many years, seems to have filled the role of 'black sheep'. While at Cambridge, gambling and drink led to serious debt and there are some contrite letters written in 1849 to his father, which also express doubts over his religious faith. Though welcomed back into his family he was, for

Emily when young

the rest of his life, a cause of much concern to his parents and elder brother. Henry was sent to Rugby School at 14 and was later articled to a solicitor at Doncaster.

After Cambridge

Llewelyn had already made a name for himself as a scholar with his translation, jointly with David Vaughan, of Plato's *Republic*. Theirs was one of the standard translations for many years and appeared in the *Golden Treasury* edition. He was also beginning to become known as an Alpine mountaineer. But his future, like that of 50% of graduates at the time (according to Gladstone), was to be in the Church. Llewelyn was ordained at Durham in 1851 and worked first as Curate at St. Anne's, Limehouse and then as Vicar at St. Mark's, Whitechapel, both being very poor parishes in London's East End. In 1856 he was appointed Rector of Christ Church, Marylebone, a position he held until 1889, when he would move North to Kirkby Lonsdale.

Not long after Llewelyn was settled in Marylebone, tragedy struck the family. First Jane and then Henry were taken ill with tuberculosis. After several years of failing health, Jane died in January 1858, and Henry in July.

In October the same year, news came from China that William, who had a naval chaplaincy, had also died. Thus, within 10 months, John and Mary Davies had lost three of their five children. When they died, their beautiful elder daughter Jane, engaged to be married, was 34; poor William was 30; and the youngest, Henry, was only 25.

The effect on the family of this tragic year can only be imagined. Llewelyn, it seems, sought solace in his beloved Switzerland, and it was in September of this same year that he made the first ascent of the Dom. This achievement brought

Jane in 1851
(drawing by Annabella Mason)

him an honoured place in Alpine history. [For his account of the climb see Appendix A.]

The other surviving child, Emily, remained at Gateshead with her parents until the death of her father in 1861. Mrs Davies and Emily then moved to London, where Llewelyn had found them a small house a short walk from his own home in Blandford Square. There is now a blue plaque on 17, Cunningham Place, in St. John's Wood, to mark the home, from 1861 until 1908, of Emily Davies, the founder of Girton, the first women's college in Cambridge.The plaque was unveiled in January 1978 by the Labour peer Pat Llewelyn Davies, daughter-in-law of Crompton Llewelyn Davies. My mother, Theodora, my sister Mary and I were present on the occasion.

Emily Davies and Girton College

Emily's life work as a pioneer for the education of women, which culminated in the establishment of Girton College, has given her a well-earned place in history.

17 Cunningham Place

This is well documented in several publications, and details of the latest biography are given in the Bibliography. Her niece Margaret, two great nieces, one great great niece and one great great great niece have been privileged to go to Girton as students and can justifiably feel a sense of pride in what Emily achieved all those years ago.

Girton College

Visiting the college today one cannot help wondering what she would have thought of the modern changes. In particular the sight of men students wandering along those endless corridors and enjoying the wonderful grounds still fills this great great niece with a sense of astonishment. Even in my mother's day, during the First World War, an unmarried uncle was not allowed to visit a student's room without a chaperone being present!

Girton College, now much extended, still stands at the supposedly safe distance of nearly three miles from the other Cambridge colleges. The black and white photo of the college does no justice to the relentlessly red bricks of the Waterhouse building. Round the corner to the left is the Emily Davies Court, where the author received and accepted an offer of marriage in 1955.

Emily receiving an Honorary LLD
from Glasgow University in 1902

Sir Charles & Lady Caroline Crompton and their children

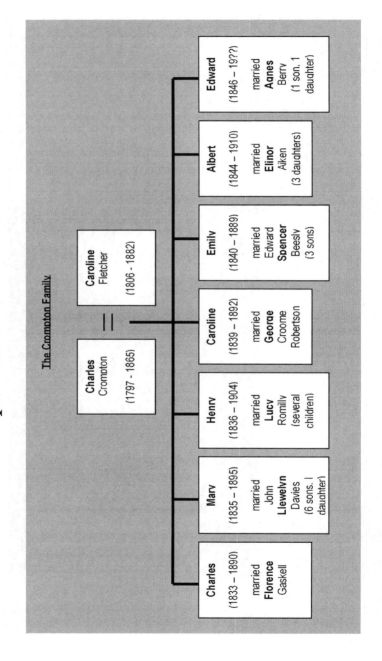

The Crompton Family

| **Charles** Crompton (1797 - 1865) | == | **Caroline** Fletcher (1806 - 1882) |

Charles (1833 – 1890)
married **Florence** Gaskell

Mary (1835 – 1895)
married John **Llewelyn** Davies (6 sons, 1 daughter)

Henry (1836 – 1904)
married **Lucy** Romilly (several children)

Caroline (1839 – 1892)
married **George** Croome Robertson

Emily (1840 – 1889)
married Edward **Spencer** Beesly (3 sons)

Albert (1844 – 1910)
married **Elinor** Aiken (3 daughters)

Edward (1846 – 19??)
married **Agnes** Berry (1 son, 1 daughter)

2 The Crompton Family

Watercolour of Mary Crompton aged 2

Mary Crompton was born in 1834, the eldest daughter of Sir Charles Crompton QC, a judge of the Queen's Bench, and Lady Caroline Crompton.

The Crompton family can be traced back to 1242, and there were branches in East Yorkshire, Lancashire and Derbyshire. According to the Dictionary of National Biography, the Cromptons were 'of Yorkshire Puritan stock and connected with the Cheshire family of Bradshaw the regicide.' My mother was fond of telling the story that Charles Crompton, when asked if there had been a judge in the family before, used to reply "Yes, and he sentenced a great criminal," referring to the fact that John Bradshaw, the regicide, presided at the trial of Charles I and his was the first signature on the death warrant. It is said that he was the only judge prepared to play this role. Bradshaw was buried in Westminster Abbey and was later exhumed, together with Oliver Cromwell and Henry Ireton, and their bodies were hung up for public display and derision.

Unfortunately, as was the case with James Davies's claim to be descended from Llewelyn, Prince of Wales, it seems that John Bradshaw had no legitimate issue. But his brother certainly did, so there may be a connection, if not a straight line of descent.

The Crompton parents

Much research has been done by genealogists on the various branches of the Crompton family, but I do not intend to explore beyond Mary's own parents, Sir Charles and Lady Caroline Crompton. Sir Charles died in 1865, the year after my grandfather Maurice, the fourth child, had been born at Eardiston, his grandparents' house in Worcestershire. [See Bibliography for details of a sketch book of that memorable visit.] Soon after her husband's death Lady Crompton left Eardiston and bought Chorley Hall, near Bridgnorth in Shropshire. In so doing she became 'Lady of the Manor of Chorley'. The grandchildren enjoyed many happy holidays with her at Chorley, and it was from there that her youngest daughter, Emily, was married in 1869. Caroline Crompton clearly lived at Chorley Hall for part of the year, but she also had a house in London, where the 1871 census finds the family at 23 Westbourne Terrace. Caroline Crompton outlived her husband by 18 years and was nursed for some months before she died in 1882 at her daughter Mary's home in Dorset Square, Marylebone, where the Llewelyn Davies family were living at the time.

After Lady Crompton's death, Chorley Hall passed to her eldest son, Charles and, after his death in 1890, to the next son, Henry. Each brother in turn enjoyed the title 'Lord of the Manor' during his period as owner of Chorley Hall. The Llewelyn Davies family continued to visit Chorley, although this was clearly not so popular with their father. In writing to Theodore in 1884, Llewelyn says: 'I wonder where we shall go in the Summer. Your mother seems to think that Chorley is our fate.' The house remained in the Crompton family until 1934.

Uncles and aunts

Mary had four brothers and two sisters who all, in their different ways, had an important influence on the lives of the Llewelyn Davies family. Her much loved elder brother Charles married the novelist Elizabeth Gaskell's eldest daughter Florence, but they had no children. Charles Crompton was a lawyer who became a QC and later a Liberal MP, the member for Leek in Staffordshire He was a devoted uncle to the seven Llewelyn Davieses. His letter to Arthur on his engagement to Sylvia du Maurier refers to 'that happiest of families.' And, when he was dying, his nephew Crompton Llewelyn Davies wrote to Sylvia du Maurier: 'You do not know what Uncle Charley has been to us all.'

Mary's second brother Henry was a barrister and a leading figure in the Positivist movement. [For something about Positivism, see chapter 15.] He strongly supported Trades Unionism, which was unfashionable at the time. He and his wife Lucy Romilly had several children of whom one, a son Paul, was tragically drowned with his wife and six children when the Lusitania was torpedoed in 1915.

Albert, Mary's third brother, was also a prominent Positivist. He invited his nephew, Maurice Llewelyn Davies, my grandfather, to join his shipping firm in Liverpool, Alfred Holt & Co (the Blue Funnel Line), where Maurice soon became a director. This is where my grandfather spent his working life. Albert and his wife Nelly had several daughters but she died quite young after an operation.

Edward, Uncle Ned, the youngest of Mary's brothers, fulfilled a similar role by giving his nephew Harry Llewelyn Davies a job for life. Edward was an engineer at Cochran & Co, which started as a small firm of shipbuilders and boiler makers in Birkenhead. This was where Edward, who was a partner in the firm, designed the revolutionary vertical boiler, illustrated on page 77.

Edward Crompton.

This boiler soon became famous throughout the world and, in 1898, the firm moved to Annan in Dumfriesshire. Harry soon rose to be the Managing Director and Chairman. Edward and his wife Agnes had a son and a daughter.

It was Edward and Albert who, travelling on the Continent in their youth, observed one of their fellow guests trying to decipher words from the blotter in the hotel lounge with the use of a mirror. They waited until no-one was around, wrote on a clean sheet of paper the words "I have disposed of the body but cannot think what to do with the head", and blotted it, before removing the paper. History does not relate what happened next. The same two, arriving at a small hotel in Germany, registered their names: 'Elector of Middlesex' and 'Elector of Westminster'. They were treated with the utmost respect during their stay.

Of Mary's two sisters, Caroline was the last to marry. Her husband was Professor George Croome Robertson, a distinguished philosopher, much concerned with women's suffrage. Caroline too was a great supporter of Emily Davies and acted as College Secretary during the years which covered the move to Girton from Hitchin, where the college first opened.

Uncle George and Aunt Carry had no children and were popular visitors at the Llewelyn Davies home. Meta Muir, a friend of Margaret's from Girton days, staying with the family at the same time as Uncle George and Aunt Carry, described the professor as 'full of fun and jokes' in a letter to her sister. She went on:

> 'Nothing could be more delightful than our talk at table – a mixture of chat and seriousness, never too much of either, for after the wise ones have been talking strikes and economy or philosophy for a little while, Mr. C.R. always gives the conversation a turn and makes it general again.'

The younger sister, Emily, married Professor E.S. Beesly, the brother of Augustus Beesly who taught at Marlborough during the time that the boys were there and was Housemaster to some of them. Spencer Beesly was Principal of one of the colleges within London University where they lived in Gordon Square.

There is an account of Emily and Spencer's wedding at Stottesdon Parish Church near Chorley in July 1869 in a letter from Charley, then aged nine, to his Grandmamma Davies [see chapter 7]. Margaret, who was not quite eight, also wrote a few weeks later when the newly weds were staying with them at Chorley. I am including the letter here as it contains a nice reference to the children's new Uncle Spencer:

Dear Grandmamma,

I hope you are pretty well. Charley and Arthur and I are learning to shoot with bows and arrows. There are two targets and first we shoot at one and then at the other. We go sometimes into the Farmer's rickyard and there is all loose straw and we tumble about in it, and slip down and we play at I spy there, and have such fun. Little baby [probably Crompton] likes to walk in the chaff and the straw very much. He is much better than he was. He roars so when he may not go into the garden.

Spencer Beesly

Uncle Spencer is so kind as to look over the boy's [sic] Latin exercises. I think it's a great honour to have a Professor to teach them. We have got a great map that we may find the places where Mamma & Papa are going to. Charley is learning carpentering from an old man called Richard Wall who has helped him to make 2 stools and a little waggon.

Goodbye, from your affectionate Margaret C. Davies

[No Latin or carpentry lessons for the little girl. Richard Wall is listed in Kelly's Directory for 1870 as a local wheelwright. The recently refurbished Chorley Hall, pictured below, is today called 'Chorley Manor'.]

Emily died in 1889 at the age of 49, leaving Spencer and three sons. Mary went to London to help nurse her during her last weeks.

So, for the Llewelyn Davies children as they grew up, there was a profusion of Crompton uncles, aunts and cousins. This was in sad contrast to the Davies side of the family where, through the ravages of tuberculosis, there was only Aunt Emily, who never married.

3 The Marriage of Llewelyn and Mary

Llewelyn became engaged to Mary Crompton in the Spring of 1859. We do not know how they met, but it may well have been through one of Mary's brothers, involved as they were in similar liberal interests as Llewelyn. His sister Emily records how, when she was staying with Llewelyn at that time, he went to visit Mr Sheppard, a former Repton master. Mrs Sheppard told Emily afterwards that she had asked him what flower Mary was like, mentioning one after another, to all of which he said "No." 'But presently (he) went into the garden and, bringing in a white pink, said "She is like that."' In *The Morgue*, Peter Llewelyn Davies commented: 'The pretty little story of Llewelyn and the white pink is literally the only piece of sentiment in the whole of ED's *Chronicle*.'

Mary as a young woman

A small insight into Mary's feelings at this time appeared in a letter written years later to her daughter Margaret, who had herself had a proposal of marriage in June 1889:

> 'I remember well how everybody seemed to me just <u>impossible</u> till JLl.D came on the scene – and then, tho' at times awful qualms and horrors assailed me when he was out of my sight, whenever I was with him and felt all the strength and comfort of his presence, my way seemed clear and I knew that, if I gave up, the best happiness of my life wd. be gone.'

Llewelyn and Mary were married on 13 September 1859 at the tiny parish church at Llanstinan in Pembrokeshire where the Crompton parents were living at the time. The wedding was conducted by Llewelyn's father, the Rev. John Davies. Llewelyn was 34 and Mary nine years younger. Emily recorded:

> 'It was a pouring wet day. The bride and bridegroom reached home first and had lighted a fire by the time the rest of the party arrived.'

What a delightfully informal scene that conjures up, even if we know full well that it will have been a servant who lit the fire!

After a short tour in North Wales, they settled in Milton Street, Dorset Square, in the house in which Llewelyn had lived for a few years as a lodger.

Llanstinan Church

Before the birth of their first child they moved round the corner to 18 Blandford Square, where all but two of their children would be born.

Mary and Llewelyn came from very different backgrounds. The Davies parents' strict Evangelical views and the austere if kindly atmosphere in which Llewelyn grew up, compounded by the tragic loss of a sister and two brothers in one year, must surely have left their mark on him. Three years after their deaths, in 1861, his father died and he was left with just one younger sister and a widowed mother. It is scarcely surprising that he felt his family responsibilities keenly and appeared somewhat reserved and austere. Mary, on the other hand, came from a happy and more carefree family, and life had not yet dealt them any serious traumas. What is evident is that, together, Llewelyn and Mary formed an extremely strong partnership.

Peter Llewelyn Davies observed:

> 'I have no idea what he was like as a father to his children or as a husband
> to his wife. As a father I merely guess him to have been pretty strict, while
> I think it is clear that Mary Ll.D contributed warmth and deep affection
> to the domestic scene. Between them they brought up six sons and a
> daughter without a single black sheep among them – no small achieve-
> ment.'

It seems to me that Llewelyn was fully as devoted to his children as was their
mother, although he was not so effusive in his expression of this devotion
as she was. There are examples of them both, often with one voice, saying
firmly what was and what was not acceptable or advisable. This might have
been instructions to Theodore away at school that he should not eat
biscuits; or warning him about the danger of reading too many novels for
fear of becoming addicted to the practice. All
the children were clearly guided by their parents and grew up with the greatest respect for
their judgment. Mary was always ready to
advise on practical matters, and this advice
appears to have been heeded, even when her
children were older.

An example of this comes in Harry's letter to
Theodore ['Dearest Chubby', see chapter 11],
enclosing a birthday present. He mentions
that he has had a bad cold and 'Mother would
not let me go out of doors.' He was 17 at the
time. Her letters to Margaret as a young adult
are full of recommendations and instructions.
As for Llewelyn, I can well imagine that a   "those piercing eyes"
piece of advice or even a solemn word from him would be quite enough to
convey his view without any need for more. Those piercing blue eyes, which
dominate the few photographs we have of him, say it all. The dying Arthur,
in the letter included in Chapter 9, addressed his father as 'a brave and wise
man' and this seems to have been how he was perceived in the family.

In a short account of Margaret, written in 1944 shortly after her death,
Crompton Llewelyn Davies's daughter Katharine describes the Llewelyn
Davies household. She must have been given this impression by her father,
since she herself was born 20 years after Mary died:

> 'The whole family breathed an atmosphere of advanced liberal thought
> and a high sense of social responsibility. John Llewelyn Davies … was not
> rich, his sons having to earn their education by scholarships, and being, as
> one of them afterwards expressed it: "little struggle-for-lifers". But the
> household possessed a wealth of grace from the influence of his wife,
> Mary Crompton. Everyone who met her fell under the charm of her
> personality; her children adored her and, on the last day of the holidays,
> would follow her round from room to room as she did their packing,

unable to bear being out of her sight for an instant. Well educated herself, she read French and Latin with them and, as they grew up, continued to share their interests and was repaid by undiminished comradeship and devotion on their part.'

There is a further glimpse of Mary when she was in her fifties from Dolly Ponsonby, a close family friend, who became ill with jaundice at the age of 14 while staying with the Llewelyn Davieses at Kirkby Lonsdale in 1890:

> 'Mrs Davies's kindness was unforgettable. (She) would bring me up grapes and ice. The house seemed perfectly run with a real feeling of home – fires and nice servants in caps, and particularly good food – and I remember my mother taking away some receipts of old-fashioned puddings. But Mrs Llewelyn Davies was not only a perfect housewife, but a woman with a remarkable brain, and great knowledge and love of literature and poetry....
>
> To me she transmuted what had hitherto appeared rather dry and difficult poems into things of interest and excitement and beauty – reading aloud so well and naturally, explaining any difficult parts or words so simply. I especially remember being thrilled by her reading after tea in the drawing room, Matthew Arnold's 'Sohrab and Rustum'.

Sadly, Mary's health was poor in middle age and the nature of her illness is not at all clear. It has been suggested that it was the result of having seven children in ten years, and a comment by Dr. Elizabeth Garrett Anderson, recorded in one of Margaret's commonplace books, confirms that the babies did follow rather too rapidly on each other for comfort:

> ' "Poor Mrs Ll.D has just confessed to me that there is another baby coming. But I patted her on the back and said 'Never mind, my dear, good breed, good breed." '

However, the intermittent nature of her recurrent incapacity suggests that it might have been something more like multiple sclerosis. She was confined to her bed and in pain for a week at a time and, after one of these attacks, would find walking difficult and be weak enough to use a Bath Chair. Yet, between bouts, she sounds vigorous and well able to go visiting and to travel around. These problems certainly started several years before Theodore went to Marlborough, as she mentions in writing to him that she misses him popping in to see her when she is confined to bed, and walking alongside her Bath Chair. She is described as 'very poorly' in a letter

from Arthur in 1880, fifteen years before her death from a stroke in 1895, at the age of 61.

It would be interesting to know what household duties Mary herself performed. When convalescing in Brighton after one of her 'attacks' in September 1883, she wrote that she was enjoying not having to 'order dinners', which suggests she did little cooking herself. On the other hand, there is a description of how she and Harry spent the afternoon re-potting jam sent from Chorley which had leaked in transit from its original jam jars. The census of 1871, when all seven children were still at home, with Crompton aged three and Theodore only one, lists two 'nurses' [or as we should call them 'Nannies'], as well as a cook and a housemaid. A coachman, Henry Dawson, is mentioned a number of times and was with the family in Worcestershire in 1864 when Maurice was born. There is reference too to a boy, or 'attendant', who may have helped in the garden and with odd jobs. One can imagine that all four living-in servants took a part in the upbringing of the children, especially when their mother was laid up. In a letter written to Theodore, the last to leave home, in his first few weeks at Marlborough, his mother wrote:

> 'Mrs W. is rather lonely, and declares the Nursery looks like another room now you are gone. But she is making me a dress wh. occupation comforts her.'

Mary wrote to Theodore, then aged 13, in March 1883 during a spell of illness:

> 'I am looking forward hopefully to my breakfast tray tomorrow morning. "Letters from all my dear boys" I shall say, as dear Pa bears it in.'

Again, a nice picture of 'the bearded clergyman' as he was described by Matthew Arnold in a letter written in September 1858. This suggests that more conventional clergy at that period were clean-shaven. Another glimpse of Llewelyn's involvement in domestic matters was in September 1887 when Mary, writing to Margaret, told how she had been incapacitated by a bad headache: 'but Papa, when he returned from a funeral, got me tea early which had its usual good effect.'

Throughout the letters that survive are remarks that show Llewelyn and Mary to have been a very devoted couple. 'We are very snug together' is a comment Mary uses a number of times, including in her last letter to Margaret, written the day before she died.

4 Blandford Square and Christ Church

Blandford Square

The Llewelyn Davies family lived at 18 Blandford Square in Marylebone, London, for 20 years. This was conveniently placed a couple of minutes' walk from Christ Church, where Llewelyn was Rector, the Church having no rectory of its own. From various comments, Blandford Square seems to have been a typical London square of terrace houses, built on the site of some botanical gardens in the 1830s, round a pleasant garden presumably of mature trees and plants. Though the name is still there, redevelopment around Marylebone station involved the demolition of all the old houses, and Blandford Square, as such, no longer exists.

16 Blandford Square

Of particular interest is the fact that, from 1860, when the Llewelyn Daviesies moved there, until 1864, the novelist George Eliot lived at number 16, two doors away. Living as she was with George Lewes, then a married man, it was impossible for Mary to call on her, being a loyal Rector's wife. Unconventional the family may have been in some respects but not unconventional enough for that. Mary greatly admired George Eliot's work and, by this date, both *The Mill on the Floss* and *Adam Bede* had been published. She would dearly have liked to call on her but had to content herself with touching the front gate as she walked by. Some years later, it is interesting to note, Emily Davies established some kind of relationship with George Eliot who supported various aspects of her work. But they never became close friends.

The family moved to a slightly larger house a few streets away (no. 34 Dorset Square) in 1879, as the children got older. After my disappointment of finding no Blandford Square worthy of the name, I was most relieved to find Dorset Square round the corner. The cradle of the Marylebone Cricket Club, it was looking pleasantly Spring-like and rather prosperous, though only some fifty yards behind Marylebone station. Number 34 is an imposing four-storey Georgian house with a newly painted green front door and shiny brass fittings. One could see attic rooms and a basement too, providing plenty of room for a family of nine with several servants, as well as Mary's mother and her nurse for a time. They stayed there for three years and then the opportunity arose to acquire number 5 Blandford Square from Barbara

Bodichon, a close associate of Emily Davies's in founding Girton. This was a slightly smaller house but, by this time, Charley, Arthur and Maurice had all left home and Grandmother Crompton had died. The family moved into number 5 and remained there for the next seven years, until leaving for Kirkby Lonsdale in 1889.

Christ Church

Christ Church itself still stands on the corner of Cosway St. and Shroton St. and the building looks very well cared for.

Built between 1822 and 1825, it was redesigned by Thomas Hardwick who had studied architecture in Italy. It was a large, imposing church in classical Italian style built mainly in Bath stone, recently made available in London by the opening of the

34 Dorset Square in 2007

Kennet and Avon Canal. The building was sold in 1980 and, after restoration, was converted into sound studios and office accommodation. The engraving of Shepherd's drawing shows Christ Church in 1825. Although originally built for a socially privileged congregation, the area around the church changed drastically during the second half of the nineteenth century.

The advent of the canals and railway and the building of Marylebone Station left a trail of desolation as prosperous Georgian squares and whole streets, many with rows of attractive houses, were demolished.

With the potato famine, a great many poor Irish families moved into the small houses around Christ Church and, at the same time, many better off, professional families moved out of central London. The parish was a huge one and included the Lisson Grove quarter, one of the most deprived parts of London at that time.

So large was the area served by Christ Church that, in 1863, Llewelyn instigated the building of a subsidiary church nearby, St. Barnabas, which served the people in the district around Bell Street, towards the Edgware Road. This was demolished some thirty years later to make room for Bell St. School.

Christ Church, Marylebone

5 Early Years & Family Life

The Llewelyn Davieses were evidently not a typical Victorian family, nor were their parents typical Victorian parents. Llewelyn wrote to his youngest son, Theodore, then aged twelve: 'You cannot think what a happiness it is to have so many good and loving children.' Letters to him from the children when either he or, more often, they were away from home were chatty and affectionate, as were those they wrote to each other and the profusion of letters they sent to their mother.

One can only glean what family life was like for the children before they left home from the odd letter that survives, from Peter Davies's notes on Emily's '*Chronicle*' and from one or two comments Emily herself made in letters to her friends. Writing to Anna Richardson in 1865, she wrote: 'The little Davieses grow in wisdom and stature and loveliness.' Again, in 1867, she reported that 'Mary and the children are in Shropshire with Lady Crompton, exuberant with health and enjoyment'. And the same year, once more to her friend Anna, when Charley will have been seven and a half, Margaret six, Arthur five, Maurice three and a half and Harry two, Emily wrote:

> 'Our children seem to be pulling thro' their coughs pretty well. They were in great force on Sunday, clinging & shouting & dancing round Mr. Maurice. Even the poor baby, who is the most pulled down, cd. point to the picture on the wall when asked "Where is Mr. Maurice?" They are taught to adore the image of the prophet before they can speak...'

This reference to Frederick Denison Maurice, the founder of Christian Socialism, who had such a profound influence on their father, suggests he was a popular visitor to the house. My grandfather, Maurice, was called after him. His admirers used to refer to him as 'The Prophet.'

Peter Llewelyn Davies observed:

> 'That the family were a high-spirited lot, and by no means the cowed children of a stern father, is suggested by an extract from one of Thomas Hughes's letters to Llewelyn, undated, but probably written in the seventies: "Your boys (whom I found at high jinks besieging and defending the big armchair in the dining-room which will have, I don't doubt, to go to the carpenter's in consequence), tell me you are going to an evening party." '

It would be interesting to know whether or not Thomas Hughes, the author of *Tom Brown's Schooldays*, a close friend of Llewelyn's and one of Charley's 'sponsors' [or godparents], approved of such 'high jinks'.

Day school

As soon as they were old enough the boys were sent as day boys to the St. Marylebone & All Souls' Grammar School, generally called Barford's after the Headmaster. This was in Cornwall Terrace, Regent's Park, a short walk from Blandford Square. Peter Llewelyn Davies wrote: 'Here began that formidable habit of prize-collecting which distinguished this generation of the family.'

They had a bit of fun at the school too, however, as shown in the following extract from reminiscences by R.S.Garnett, a contemporary at Barford's, which was published in *Blackwood's Magazine* in February 1931. The Davies Secundus who features in this story is presumably Arthur, the second Llewelyn Davies son:

> 'Amo, amas, amat, amamus, amatis…The verb amo was being conjugated round my class, but Davies Secundus, the boy who should have said "amant", had left his seat on the form and was trying to catch a bluebottle fly which was buzzing round old Bellamy's bald pate. It was a critical moment, for old Bellamy, who had been lulled to sleep by the conjugation of the verb moneo, was almost certain to wake on the cessation of our voices. So, out of turn, I said "amant". And the next boy to me followed with "amabo". For the moment we were saved. But alas! Davies Secundus, in making a futile swoop at the bluebottle, struck old Bellamy on the forehead. He started up, saw the boy running back to his seat, and, with a scarlet face, called: "Davies Secundus, stand on the form!"
>
> When, a few minutes later, the headmaster suddenly came into the room, we thought it was all up for little Llewelyn Davies. The great man, however, failed to notice him, and proceeded to the object of his visit, which was to state that a theft was suspected, and that every boy present must forthwith turn out his pockets. Long before the speech was over, Davies, catching the eye of old Bellamy, had sat down. And he was the first of any of us to get anything out of his pockets… He successively placed on the table a large snail, a piece of cheese, a bacon rind and an ivory image of some kind, as also several marbles.
>
> Other boys produced similar possessions, and the inquisition was in full swing when a man-servant arrived with the information that the Queen had sent an outrider to say that Her Majesty wished to see all the boys outside the park railings in a quarter of an hour's time. This effectively put a stop to all other activities.'

Peter Llewelyn Davies ended the account:

> 'We leave the boys of Barford's, including Davies Secundus, and presumably Davies Primus and possibly Davies Tertius too, lined up outside the school and taking off their hats as the Queen drove slowly by.'

Barford's being a boys' school, Margaret had to be educated elsewhere. We know that she and her brothers learned a considerable amount of French,

Latin and English literature from their mother, who always read aloud in the evenings. It seems likely that Margaret, who was musical and artistic, had piano and singing lessons. She is said to have had a beautiful contralto voice, and we know from various references that she sang at concerts and, as a young adult, was leader of the chorus in a performance of *Electra* at Cambridge. She may have had some lessons outside the home before moving to Queen's College, Harley Street, where her father was for a time Principal.

Affection and fun

As the only girl in the family, one can imagine that Margaret must have suffered a good deal of teasing from her brothers, but beneath it lay very strong bonds of affection. One of the noticeable features of the letters that survive is the endless use of nicknames, a custom entered into fully by their mother. That it was not popular with all members of the family is shown in a letter from Charley to Theodore in which he instructs him to 'ask Maurice what in the world he means by his insane rigmarole of nicknames.'

'Hippo'

Thus Maurice is regularly referred to as 'Hippo' and at times 'The Stalwart One'. Early photographs suggest that he was quite stockily built, although this tendency didn't last into adulthood.

Harry seems to have been called 'Hurl', and Crompton abbreviated to 'Tony' and sometimes 'Scrum'. Charles was invariably 'Charley' but also 'Chillick', and Theodore often 'Theo', sometimes 'LM' [probably 'Little Man'] and, early on, 'Chubby'.

Arthur seems largely to have escaped this particular fate, although I found one reference to 'Arty'. Margaret was generally known as 'Peg' but also, at some stage, she was nicknamed 'Little Toast'. My mother told us the story that one day Margaret got very upset during breakfast when this nickname was used. One of her brothers, and history does not relate which, picked a small slice of toast from the rack and disappeared into the garden. He reappeared a few minutes later and, with great solemnity, announced: "I have buried Little Toast". The nickname was never used again.

As well as affectionate teasing there was evidently a tremendous amount of witticism on all sides, their sense of humour most probably inherited mainly from the Crompton side of the family. However a story in Bertrand Russell's autobiography shows that Llewelyn, even in old age, did not lose his ability to see the funny side of things. Russell wrote:

'I remember him [the mathematician Louis Couturat] coming to see me in a hotel in Paris in 1905, while Mr. Davies and his daughter Margaret

...listened to his conversation. He talked without a moment's intermission for half an hour, and then remarked "the wise are those who hold their tongues". At this point Mr. Davies, in spite of his eighty years, rushed from the room, and I could just hear the sound of his laughter as he disappeared.'

Mary records in a letter that she had to advise Llewelyn not to joke too much with his children in order to keep his dignity.

6 Away at School

Marlborough College

When her father Maurice died in April 1939, my mother received the following letter. It was addressed 'To the Executors of Maurice Llewelyn Davies':

Dear Unknown,

I hope this may come to the hands of one of the daughters of Maurice Llewelyn Davies. I am his old master as I had charge of the Upper Sixth Form at Marlborough College for 36 years. I had under me all the family of boys but one, Harry, who went to Haileybury. They were a line of quite exceptionally able boys. To teach them was a duty but it became an inspiration. I owed them very much for that, and I look back now as an old man on those days of happy intercourse and friendship with them. I think it was greatly owing to their influence in the school that Marlborough boys at that time maintained such a high level of moral influence and intellectual culture. Boys teach and help one another, and that succession of brothers was a stimulus and an example of what stimulus can effect. I am deeply grateful to them and I write this to put it on record for their descendants.

Yours sincerely,

Lewis E. Upcott

This charming letter has indeed given great pleasure to descendants of the Llewelyn Davies brothers, as it was intended to do. It gives written proof – if that is needed – that there was something rather special about the family, over and above their academic ability. All the brothers, with the exception of Harry, were sent to Marlborough College where there were reduced fees for the sons of Anglican clergy. So, from February 1872 when Charley arrived until July 1888 when Theodore left, there were often two and at times three brothers at the school. All were foundation scholars and won junior scholarships; all except Maurice were senior scholars and college prefects as well; Arthur and Crompton played in the College 1st Rugby XV.

It is difficult to know how much the boys enjoyed their time at Marlborough. Certainly the letters home from Arthur, of which a large number written in his early years away still exist, sound cheerful enough. But the fact that none of the four brothers who had sons chose to send them there is significant. Maurice is the only one on record as having expressed dislike of the school and having said that he would never send his son Roland there. A possible factor might be that, not being sons of the clergy, none of the next generation would have qualified for reduced fees. And of course we shall never know whether Charley and Theodore, had they had sons, would have sent them to the College. A cousin, Harry Fletcher, was a contemporary of Theodore's at Marlborough and a close friend later of both Crompton and Theodore at Cambridge. His daughter, Janet Pott, in a short account of the Fletcher and Llewelyn Davies families over five generations, wrote of her father:

> 'He didn't think much of the public school spirit – cold baths, discipline etc. Did he join his Llewelyn Davies cousins at playing marbles as a protest against compulsory games?'

This throws a slightly different light on the interest of at least some of the brothers in cricket, rugby, fives and swimming and, in the case of several of them, their sporting achievements. Perhaps it was the fact that games were compulsory that fired this rebellious streak in the younger ones.

Surely, although they counted the days until the holidays, this was only natural coming as they did from a happy and loving home. I'm sure that, like other children away at school, there were aspects they liked and other aspects they didn't, and teachers they got on with and others they disliked. But I have found no mention that any of the brothers suffered unduly from home-sickness.

There seems to have been quite a lot of freedom so that, for example, Arthur was able to go for walks frequently with Charley. Also, throughout their time there, the younger ones enjoyed being allowed to sit in their elder brother's study, when the elder one was senior enough to have earned that privilege. Cold baths would not have struck the Llewelyn Davies boys as anything out of the ordinary. There was a theory that their mother took a cold bath each morning, though I haven't been able to verify this and it certainly doesn't sound likely later on when her health was so erratic. Swimming out-of-doors whatever the weather was a passion of Arthur's and some of the others, and this seems to have been allowed before breakfast once the boys had learned to swim.

Marlborough College

Haileybury

Haileybury

As was mentioned above, Harry alone of the brothers was sent to Hailey-bury. This was recognised as having less stringent academic requirements than Marlborough and being therefore better suited to his abilities which were rather different.

Once he had settled down, which seems to have taken a while, Harry was extremely happy for the four years he was there and it was clearly the right decision. There was a reduction in fees for sons of Church of England clergy as at Marlborough. This was fortunate as, unlike his brothers, he did not contribute to the family finances by winning scholarships. He played for the School Cricket 2nd XI during his last year at Haileybury.

7 Sketch of Charley

Charles Llewelyn Davies, Charley, was born on 29 June 1860, just nine months after his parents' marriage. The first child in any family is said to have advantages that no subsequent children can have, enjoying the undivided attention of their parents. Charley was in this privileged position for just 16 months before the appearance of Margaret on the scene, with Arthur arriving 16 months after that and the other four in rapid succession.

Charley

Early years

Perhaps because he was her first nephew, Charley seems to have held a special place in the affections of his Aunt Emily Davies. She refers to him a number of times in letters to her friend Anna Richardson. When he was three she wrote:

'It is a superstitious fancy, but I cannot help being frightened about Charley. He really does seem to me 'too good to live', tho' I dare say he is not so much sweeter & more loveable than other people's nephews, if one knew them as well. As a simple fact I never see any little child to be compared to him ....'

And, when he was a little older: 'Charley is the sweetest little child I ever saw, so gentle and tenderhearted.' Some undated lines from Charley to his father, entitled '*A Witty Letter to Papa*', were written when he was six or seven, judging from the writing and the fact that he signed it from himself and Margaret. The children were staying with their Crompton grandmother at Chorley, near Bridgnorth in Shropshire. Llewelyn had evidently injured his toe:

At number 18 Blandford Square
Lives my most belovèd Pa.
You the most beloved
Of men on this our earth,
Quite full of joyous pleasure
And also of righteous mirth.
We were so very sorry
About the mishap of the toe
And we did cry so,
Oh! Oh!!!

Tomorrow is Sunday
You're coming on Monday,
And we shall be very glad,
For to be without you so long
I am sure is bad.
And now this very short
Letter is done,
And we are going
To have some fun.

C.Ll.D and M.C.D

In Charley's earliest letters he often signed from himself and Margaret, as in the poem above, suggesting they were even then very good friends. I have an early very scuffed scrapbook too inscribed by him with both their initials.

In the summer of 1869, when he was nine, Charley wrote the following two letters to his Davies grandmother, when the children were staying at Chorley with Grandmother Crompton. In the first one he describes the wedding of Mary's youngest sister, his aunt Emily Crompton, which took place from there at Stottesdon Parish Church nearby. She married Professor Spencer Beesly, the brother of Augustus Beesly, the Marlborough master and poet, who became a big feature of some of the brothers' time at school:

Dear Grandmamma,

We hope you are pretty well. Mamma and Aunt Carry have just begun a night school for boys over 12 who work and don't go to school. There were nine boys here the first night. Two of them were 19 years old.

On the wedding day we were very much exited [sic]. We all had very fine clothes on and Aunt Emily looked very pretty. His [the bridegroom's] brother was here and he was Mr. Augustus B. and he had magnificent mustachos. When the service was over C.LlD signed his name in two great books. There were two flys with blue postilions [sic] and one little omnibus. There were twenty one people at the breakfast and it was all cold and very delicious. There were no potatoes. When Aunt Emily and Uncle Spencer went away in the afternoon we threw old shoes after their carriage and some went in. We found it so dull when all the wedding guests were gone. We had splendid triumphal arches made by the farmers and people.

Arthur lolls about on the settee and kicks up his legs when he is reading. There is a very nice lady here called Mrs. Mackenzie who wears lace gloves in the evening. She is English and lives in Rome. In the evening of the 24th there were some splendid fire works, rockets, squibs, roman candles, crackers, catherine wheels and jack in the boxes.

Margaret has got a brooch which is a dove flying and a gold locket for her bridesmaid's presents. She went to Bridgnorth on Thursday for the first time and she liked it very much. Have you ever been there? We hope you will write us a letter back again. We shall be very glad when Papa comes for a night on Monday. We have not seen him for such a long time. Aunt Carry and he and Mamma and Uncle Harry are going to Venice, I think. Do you think you will miss him? I liked the stamps Aunt Emily [Davies] sent very much indeed.

Ever yours C. Ll. Davies and M.C. Davies

It was indeed the case that Charley 'signed his name in two big books.' The marriage certificate lists him as one of the three witnesses, along with the bride's elder brother Charles and her sister Caroline. Remarkable at the age of nine!

The second letter was written a week or so later after his parents had left for their trip to Venice:

Dearest Grandmamma,

Uncle Spencer and Aunt Emily came here the day before yesterday, because Grandmamma was all alone except us. They have just come home from their wedding tour to the Lakes at Coniston. I dare say you know it. They have both been photographed at Ambleside and the photographs are very good indeed. It is very hot indeed today so I came indoors to write to you. Perhaps I told you that we are going (with Uncle Albert's help) to make a rockery and we have transplanted a great many ferns for it. If you like I will bring you a little one for your garden. Mamma sent me a little book to find the names of them. I have got a little garden and there are oaks and other trees and geraniums and I have nearly finished my mustard and cress.

We have been a ride in a cart going to fetch corn and the boys were so careless and the cart was rickety and joggy and we nearly ran over a poor old gleaner woman who went almost into the hedge. Afterwards, when the cart came into the field, we went to the coal pits and I got some ferns and had a swing. We saw two men come up on a small teatray clinging to a chain and a great many parcels of coal. Yesterday Uncle Spencer caught a great many harvest bugs and put one of them under a microscope. They are so small as to be almost invisible and of a bright scarlet colour. Under a microscope it is exactly like a large crab. The night school does not go on now and we moved all the things into a cupboard.

One day we had a peach for tea. They are just beginning to get ripe and there are hardly any gooseberries now. Uncle Ned came here on Saturday to spend Sunday with us and he is going away today. We caught some little water insects about an inch long in our bathes and put it under the microscope where it looks like a snake with a man's head.

We hope to hear from the travellers today. I have written Mamma a letter. I hope you are pretty well now. Give my love to Aunt Emily.

Ever yours affectly.

Charles Llewelyn Davies

I have quoted the two letters in full because they seem to me to give rather a good picture of Charley at this young age. He was clearly highly intelligent and amazingly articulate but also, which was more unusual in one so young, concerned about the feelings of others. Imagine him sitting indoors to write a long letter to his grandmother when so much of interest to him was going on in the house and garden.

A year earlier, Emily Davies had written, again to Anna Richardson:

> 'Charley's present hobby is collecting foreign postage stamps. He complains that, when he thinks he has got a new one, Papa says it is the same as the old one, only faded. He assured me that Papa did not believe anything, but added the reservation that "he believes in his Church things, but he does not believe that putting stuff on your head will stop you from being bald."'

Marlborough and Cambridge

Charley led the way in achieving outstanding academic success both at school and at Cambridge. At Marlborough he was a Foundation Scholar and also won Junior and Senior Scholarships, and was a College Prefect. He won a major scholarship to Trinity College, Cambridge, where he was a Bell scholar, got a first class degree in Classics and, in 1883, was awarded a fellowship. He overlapped with both Margaret and Arthur at Cambridge and there is mention in Arthur's letters of them seeing a lot of each other, such as regularly having lunch together on Sundays. Arthur reassured his mother that she needn't worry about Charley having enough exercise as 'he plays fives several times a week and ... goes out a walk on the other days.' There is mention too that Charley joined in some dancing at a Girton entertainment while Arthur, being less keen on 'female sociabilities' [and perhaps on dancing], watched from the sidelines. Charley was summoned back from London in May week to take Margaret to the Trinity Ball. In an undated letter to Margaret, probably written a few years earlier, their mother refers to her as Charley's 'special chum.'

We do not know whether Charley ever had a serious friendship which might have led to marriage. At the time when both Arthur and Maurice were engaged, their mother expressed the wish, in writing to Margaret: '...if only Charley would catch the infection!' Although, early on, he shared his London home with some of his brothers, I have found no mention of other relationships.

I have no letters from Charley as an adult, apart from the congratulatory note he wrote from Cambridge to Theodore when his youngest brother had won a Junior Scholarship at Marlborough. This is quoted in Chapter 13. But one can get an idea of the kind of man he was and the place he filled in the family, from mentions of him in some of Mary's letters to Theodore as a young boy. From these it is clear that Charley was a great favourite with his mother.

After Cambridge

Charley stayed on at Trinity for some time, doing a bit of teaching. We know he coached some Newnham girls successfully, although he was disappointed that they only gained third class degrees. He then travelled in Europe more than once tutoring a student, a practice common among graduates as a cheap way of seeing the world. On 9 March 1883, while Charley was with Farrer, his student at the time, in the South of France, his mother wrote to Theodore: :

> 'Another delicious letter from our Charley last night written "on an eminence between Mentone & Monaco." He is most kind in keeping us up in all he is doing & enjoying. He has been over for the day to Bordighera to visit our friends the Mount-Temples & the George Mac-Donalds, who inhabit there, and said he was most kindly received at both places. When he bid adieu to Mr. G. MacD., he asked C. if he was a "verse reader" and offered him a vol of his own poems & C. had the satisfaction of remarking that he knew several of them already! In fact he had set some of them to young Farrer to turn into Latin verse! They talk of setting their faces homewards in less than 3 weeks – happy thought to me! & they propose to return via Genoa, Milan, the Italian Lakes & Switzerland. Lucky fellows, are they not? But young Farrer apparently cares more for Lawn Tennis than all the scenery in the world!'

On his return Charley stayed at home for some weeks, reading for his fellowship. On 24 June 1883 Mary wrote to Theodore:

> 'Dear Charley is still here, & we hope to keep him to the end of next week. He is in very good spirits & has been so full of jokes & "wit" as quite to cut out Arthur this time!'

This distinction between 'jokes' and 'wit' is an interesting one, but difficult to assess at such a distance of time. All the boys certainly were credited with being witty. In Charley's case we know from Margaret's commonplace books that he was a great one for recounting jokes and funny stories, as she was herself. In her case these were often comic remarks made by young children. She has included several moderately amusing stories which she attributes to Charley.

The following Spring he was again touring Europe with a pupil. Mary wrote to Theodore on 11 February 1884:

> 'I was hoping to hear from Chillick [Charley] tonight, but it is past 9, so I fear the chance is over. He is to move on from Cannes on Wednesday to a place called Grasse, about half an hour inland by rail, all among the mountains. They are to join Mr. Cross there – the husband of George Eliot, wh. will be pleasant. C. says his bathing in the blue Mediterranean is one of the most delightful parts of his time out there. I expect he will look so strong and well when he comes home.'

Swimming in the Mediterranean in February would not have struck the family as anything out of the ordinary. Five days later she wrote:

> 'Good old Charley too sent me today a nice account of their removement to & settlement at Grasse. He & another gentleman made a fine across country walk from Cannes to Grasse while the lazy pupil drove & escorted the luggage! He says the country around abounds in "curious little hill fortresses, wh. no wheeled vehicle can enter & wh. remain just as they must have been in the Middle Ages or (some of them) even in Roman times.'

Career and later years

In May of the same year, after his return from Europe, Charley applied for the position of Chair of Latin at Liverpool University. His application was unsuccessful, so he changed tack and entered the Civil Service. He worked first at the Local Government Board for six years before moving to the Treasury. In 1910 he was appointed Assistant Paymaster General. On his retirement in 1919 he was given a CBE.

At first Charley and Arthur shared a house in London until Arthur went to Liverpool and subsequently got married. Later Charley welcomed the arrival of Crompton and Theodore to jobs in London and the three brothers lived together in 'a nice old house' in Barton Street, just round the corner from Westminster. During the 1914 – 1918 War, Charley moved to Lupus Street in Pimlico, where he spent the rest of his life.

He regularly enjoyed holidays in the Isle of Wight. His brothers used to laugh at him for staying in lodgings just below a cemetery and 'Charley drinks the water that flows through the graves' was a family joke. This is just one example of the affectionate teasing allotted him within the family for his mild eccentricities. Peter Llewelyn Davies, in his notes to Arthur's letters from Cambridge, describes him as 'a singularly unclubbable man' and gives this pen sketch of his uncle:

> 'In spite of his inordinate love of heat, at which fun is poked in this and other letters, I seem to remember that in his latter years he always wore a thick overcoat and muffler in London, in the height of summer. So bewrapped, he would wander up and down Charing Cross Road, scrutinising the twopenny and threepenny shelves mostly, I think; and so home to his gloomy little home in Lupus Street, Pimlico – 'Leprous Street' as Crompton and probably he himself called it, not inaptly....Was he a

melancholy or contented old bachelor, I wonder? There was a dry, humorous twist to his mouth, a twinkle in his blue eyes, and, despite his rather terrifying love of accuracy which found an outlet in reading the proofs of The London Library catalogue, as well as in totting up the pay of H.M. forces, there was a kindness about his expression which I associate with all his family.'

Peter's reference to accuracy stems from having been a recipient of his uncle's favourite observation if anyone was slipshod: "Accuracy, my dear boy, accuracy!"

Charley, with his love of books, evidently had an interest in family history. When there was an enquiry about the Rev. John Davies, Rector of Gateshead, in the *Notes & Queries* column of what appears to be a church newspaper, it was Charley who wrote in with details of his grandfather. Likewise, it was Charley who wrote a substantial seven page *In Memoriam* of his father for the *Contemporary Review* in June 1916. He also put together from his father's papers a collection of letters Llewelyn had received from interesting and eminent men of the day. He then got his nephew, Peter Llewelyn Davies, to publish them in 1925 under the title '*From a Victorian Postbag*.' [For details of this last publication, see the Bibliography.]

A few months before his death at the age of 67, Charley suffered a minor stroke. The effect of this was to enhance, according to Peter Llewelyn Davies, his 'most sensitive, gentle, kindly expression', as his face was then 'framed in fine silvery hair owing to his being unable to shave.' He died at home on 30 November 1927.

8 Sketch of Margaret

Margaret Caroline Davies was born on 16 October 1861. The second child and only girl in the family, she later dropped the Caroline and adopted the name Llewelyn that all her brothers were given as second names. She liked to be known as Margaret Llewelyn Davies.

She was to outlive her six brothers, in some cases by many years, and died in May 1944 at the age of 82. When Margaret died I was eleven so my memories of her are quite clear, although only those of a young child. When we were children she played a significant part in our lives, particularly as she and her friend Lilian Harris stayed with us in the Lake District for 14 months during the Second World War, and by then I was eight or nine. She was nearly eighty and in some ways a semi invalid. To hide her thinning hair she wore a beautifully embroidered muslin cap and, round her neck on a black velvet ribbon, a silver whistle that she used piercingly to attract the attention of Lilian who was by then deaf as well as partially sighted. I still have two of the caps and the silver whistle in my possession. She had been strikingly beautiful as a young woman and, even in old age, was very fine looking.

My sisters and I were too young to have much knowledge at all of her life work as a social reformer and pioneer of the rights of working women. [I say 'sisters' because, in the Spring of 1939, my sister Mary and I were joined by Judith Laszlo, a five year old Jewish girl who escaped by Kindertransport from Czechoslovakia. She was part of our family until her death in 2001. But that is another story.]

Leonard Woolf who, with Virginia, was a close friend, described Margaret as 'one of the most eminent women I have known' – and he had known quite a few! Certainly, when one reads about her work as the Secretary and leading light of the Women's Co-operative Guild for 32 years, there can be little doubt of her long-lasting influence.

Margaret as a young girl

When she was 14, Margaret wrote to her Grandmamma Davies while staying at Chorley with her Grandmother Crompton:

Chorley, July 16th 1876

Dearest Grandmamma,

It is a great shame that I have not written to you before, but I will try and make up now by writing you a good long one. I was glad to hear that you have been keeping moderately well through this excessively hot weather. I suppose you have had it hotter in London than we have here, if that is possible...

(Monday) Yesterday afternoon we had the most tremendous thunderstorm that I think I ever saw. The thunder began at two o'clock, and soon after some drops, quite as large as a penny, began to fall. The lightening was incessant. First in one part, then in another. Some were most beautiful flashes. Pink streaks running like a serpent all down the sky ... one seemed to have come right down to our feet. Within a second after, a tremendous clap followed, which made us all jump so. The storm would have seemed more fine if it had been in the night...

The roses this year are splendid. We have got glass ornaments in the rooms filled with the most choice of roses. Beautiful dark red ones, with the 'Gloire de Dijon' and pinky-white ones all mixed together with maiden hair. How I wish you had them on your table instead of ours! I don't see why we should have everything delightful while we are enjoying ourselves so much, and you only your horrid pain! You can't think what grand games we have at lawn tennis. "Mamma springs about as if she were 20", is always said. She enjoys the game immensely....

With much love, ever your affectionate grandchild,

Margaret C. Davies

Don't trouble yourself to answer this letter, if you don't feel up to it.

Two years at Girton

Compared with most girls of her generation Margaret was very well educated, firstly at home with her mother, probably with some lessons outside the home, then at Queen's College, Harley Street, and, finally, at Girton College, Cambridge. Like her brothers she was very hard working and passed the necessary exams to get into Girton. But, unlike her brothers, she was not, as a woman, eligible for the scholarships they won with such ease. She overlapped with Charley and Arthur at Cambridge and, by all accounts, had a lively social time. Her contemporary and close friend Rosie Nash, wrote the following description of Margaret in a memoir:

'She was a beautiful girl, full of life and gifted with great power of enjoyment, more beautiful and hardly less vital in the early years of a long old age. As a young woman she strikingly resembled Andrea del Sarto's saints portrayed from his wife, with her dark hair, good features and shapely head. Of one of her later photographs Roger Fry said: "What a perfect Greek head!" And there is another likeness in Ceres, the Romanised motherly goddess, in the Vatican. The fine contralto voice, not over heavy, was a delight to her young contemporaries. It had none of the effect of singing into a bottle that spoils some contraltos. I think of evenings at Girton when five of us used to meet in one of the very small sitting rooms and used to ask for '*Mary Morrison*' -- to a lovely air, not the traditional one – or for 'the little German song', a romantic volkslied. These especially she sang with youthful grace and feeling. Stanford praised her voice when she applied to join the Cambridge choir. But she never thought of devoting herself to music. The beautiful voice found its use in talk and an occasional speech.'

Margaret left Girton after two years without taking a degree. Reading through her mother's letters to her at this time, the emotional pressure on her from both parents to come home is very evident. As the only daughter, her duty was to be with them, especially as her mother's health was far from good. The theory that the academic work was beyond her is in my view wrong: she was both intelligent and hard-working. The letters leave me feeling grieved for Margaret and resentful on her behalf that she was subjected to this pressure.

We do not know how the founder of Girton, her Aunt Emily, reacted to the decision that Margaret should go home. But she too had had to reconcile career with filial duty, and it is most impressive how both women managed to pursue their life work, while at the same time being dutiful and devoted daughters. Mary clearly felt some guilt over Margaret leaving Girton where she was so happy. In May 1883 she wrote: 'I hope you don't feel too sorry to be leaving. I shall always know you have done it partly for me; I could really have got along very well for another year.' On 11 June she wrote:

'You are much in my thoughts, in leaving, and I know your heart will be heavy to say goodbye and to come to the end of a time you have enjoyed

so much. These two years have been a great advantage to you we shall always feel.... My mind is full of all I should like to do for and with you in the future. If only I were more capable! But no doubt there is some purpose in my incapacity – at any rate I like to think so. It may be to teach me patience and submission – and to bring out something in you – if we are unable to do all we could wish. At any rate you will be my comfort and right hand, and I am sure a great pleasure to yr. father, who has to suffer from my poor and at times depressing society!'

Life at home

To what extent Mary's expectation that, once home, Margaret would be her 'right hand' was fulfilled, is open to doubt. Certainly she must have been a great boon to her father, accompanying him on many social occasions when Mary was not well enough to go.

The following letter from Margaret to Theodore, then aged 13 and at Marlborough, written a few weeks after her return home from Girton, illustrates this, as it does her fondness for her youngest brother and her continuing fascination with thunderstorms:

5, Blandford Square, Saturday, 30 June 1883

Dearest Theo,

What hot work you must have found cricket this last day or two – but perhaps you think it is almost worse to do lessons. You can imagine how baking it has been (and is) here. Last night we had the most tremendous thunderstorm – such wonderful sheet lightening. The rain came in like fun just outside Charley's door. Papa and I went up in our nightgowns to inspect. I brought out towels and a bath etc to sop and catch the wet. We had only just got in from Lady Stanley's party where I had the honour of shaking hands with the great Robert Browning. It seems as hot as ever today and we think more rain is coming. Papa is sitting in his study with his coat off and door and window open.

Mrs Janie Fletcher came here yesterday to give an account of her Marlborough doings. She said you were looking very well – so red and brown. I hope Maurice did the affable to her well.

Charley goes off to Cambridge this afternoon – and is going to stay there for two months. So we shan't get him to Chorley till September, which is a pity.

I hope you will be pretty high in your form this week. Why shouldn't you get the form prize? I certainly think you ought – with both Maurice and Crompton at Marlbro'! Do you think Harry Fletcher will? I wonder whether you dislike long letters as much as poor Crom. used. You must remember that <u>we</u> don't share his feelings. We think you treat us rather shabbily – and don't tell us much. However we shall soon have the old Chappie home with us. And right glad shall we be to have you with us again.

Goodbye, my Theo – from your loving Sister

Co-operative work

In 1883, now re-established at Blandford Square, Margaret volunteered as a Sanitary Inspector visiting the poor homes in her father's parish of Marylebone. This work involved going into people's houses and, through talking with the families, recording in detail the conditions in which they were living and what amenities if any they had. This was an ideal training for the approach she later adopted in her work for the Women's Co-operative Guild. Mainly through the warmth of her character she would gain the trust and often the affection of the women she met. At the same time, from careful observation and, preferably, through hearing the women tell their own stories, she was able to analyse their social problems.

Then, based on this solid information, she was in a position to suggest possible solutions where she saw them and campaign for change and reform. In spite of coming from a more privileged background herself, it is clear from all the accounts of her, and also from her achievements, that she possessed a rare and unusual gift. This was the ability to establish relationships with the very poor, uneducated and underprivileged without intimidating or patronising them.

Probably through the influence of her father, Margaret became interested in the Co-operative movement. In 1886 she joined the local Co-operative Society in Marylebone, where her enthusiasm for co-operative sausages soon became a family joke.

The Co-operative Movement

The Co-operative Movement, which began in the first half of the nineteenth century, had at the start been entirely male-dominated. It grew out of the ideas of Robert Owen who had used his settlement at New Lanark to put into practice his social and educational theories. His village scheme had established mutual co-operation rather than profit as the prevailing ethos. In 1882 a woman named Mary Acland made a tour of factories in Northern England and witnessed at first hand co-operative principles in practice. Fired with enthusiasm, she persuaded the Editor of the *Co-operative News* to run a Women's Column in its January 1883 issue. As a result of this, The Women's League for the Spread of Co-operation was launched in April

1883 with Mrs Acland as Secretary and seven committee members. The objects of the League were stated as the following:

1. To spread a knowledge of the advantages of co-operation;

2. To stimulate amongst those who know its advantages a greater interest in the principles of co-operation;

3. To keep alive in ourselves, our neighbours, and especially in the rising generation, a more earnest appreciation of the value of co-operation to ourselves, our children, and to the nation;

4. To improve the conditions of women all over the country.

In September 1883 the first branch was established at Hebden Bridge, followed by branches in Rochdale and Woolwich. In August of the following year, the League was renamed the Women's Co-operative Guild.

The Women's Co-operative Guild

In 1887, when Margaret became secretary of the small Marylebone branch of the Women's Co-operative Guild, the WCG had already grown as a national organisation with branches around the country and some 1,000 members. Soon she was elected to the national executive committee and, in 1889, became its General Secretary.

Leonard Woolf, in his autobiography, wrote the following description of the Guild:

'The Women's Co-operative Guild or W.C.G. was an organization of women members of Co-operative Societies.... and its objects were 'to educate its members, advance co-operative principles, and to obtain for women's interests the recognition which within and without the movement is due to them'. It sounds dreary and superficially it was dreary, for on its surface were the drabness and cheerlessness which, not without reason, infected the working classes and their institutions at the beginning of the 20th century. In fact it was a unique and even exciting regiment of women whose energy and vitality were exhilarating.

They were almost all of them working class women who had had little or no regular education, and they were organized, in the traditional working class way, in 'Branches'—i.e. the women members of a Co-operative Society, say the York Co-operative Society, formed a York Branch of the W.C.G. which was federated with all the other branches in the Guild which had its head office in London. Each branch held its weekly, fortnightly, or monthly meetings, and sent its delegate to the Annual Congress of the Guild, held in London or Manchester or some other big town.

The vitality and inspiration of the Guild—and also its organization—were mainly due to Margaret. I think that what had primarily moved and shocked her was the grimness, hardship, narrowness of the lives to which most working class wives and mothers were condemned.

Then, when she got to know them individually and in the mass, she was deeply moved and exhilarated to find in them great strength and resilience of character, great potentialities, not merely as human beings, but also as political animals. She was that strange and usually inexplicable phenomenon 'a born leader'.

When Margaret took over as General Secretary, there was a subtle change in the direction of the Guild. This drew it closer in line with the political focus of the main Co-operative Movement, advocating closer links with Trade Unionists as well as campaigning for the enfranchisement of women. At conferences resolutions were passed in support of the Labour movement and trade unionism.

In her first *'Winter Circular'* she called for branch meetings not just to consist of discussions of sewing and baking. Rather, she exhorted Guild members, their purpose should be the spread of Co-operation which could only be achieved by educating themselves first. The annual report for 1892 reflects this more politically ambitious stance, setting forth the following 'duties' of the Guild:

1. To secure satisfactory conditions for employees;

2. To see that trades union regulations were carried out as regards wages and hours;

3. To definitely organise co-operative propaganda;

In this undated photo of a group of Guildswomen Margaret is in front on the right

4. To train members in the business side of store life, with a view to taking a more direct share in the management of societies;

5. To study municipal questions;

6. To arrange for sick benefit clubs for members;

7. To promote institutions for young people.

The move to Kirkby Lonsdale

It so happened that, in the very same year that Margaret became Secretary of the WCG, her father was appointed to the Trinity living at Kirkby Lonsdale in Westmorland. It was thought by many that this move to the remote Northern vicarage would put an end to Margaret's aspirations and work. This was far from the case. A room on the first floor of the vicarage with windows looking out over the churchyard towards the church was converted into an office.

This was always called the 'Red Room', presumably from its décor, and it was from here that the Women's Co-operative Guild was run for the next 19 years. Lilian Harris is at the further desk in the photo above. With the help of Lilian, who came from a large family in Kirkby Lonsdale and became an indispensable colleague and life-long friend, Margaret organised the Guild. She travelled frequently on WCG business but was based at the vicarage, often taking post into the town in the family wheelbarrow. Her duty to her parents, as their only daughter, was one that she never abandoned. In a *Memoir* of Margaret, her friend Rosie Nash wrote:

'During the years spent in Westmorland the sense of banishment gave her a constant heartache, though in later years she came to recognise that the move to Kirkby Lonsdale was not all loss. In those days the Southern co-operative societies were few and mostly small, but from Kirkby the large North country societies could be reached, and she could and did get to know the independent and energetic women of the textile districts.'

A further bonus was her friendship with Lilian, on whose 'steady and capable help and above all good judgment' she came to rely.'

In 1908 Llewelyn finally retired at the age of 82. Mary had died in 1895, Theodore in 1905 and Arthur in 1907. Together father and daughter moved back to London (together of course with the WCG head office) and Margaret cared for Llewelyn

Lilian and Margaret

devotedly at their home in Hampstead until his death in 1916 at the age of 90.

It was not until 1921 that Margaret retired from her post as Secretary of the WCG. By this time membership of the Guild had grown from 1,100 when she took over the job to 52,000 when she left. That statistic alone is an indication of how successful her work had been, but she achieved far more then a phenomenal growth in membership. While she was at the helm, the Guild focussed attention on the truly appalling conditions of working wives and mothers. By tireless lobbying of public health authorities and other government bodies, the Guild proposed and carried through huge changes

in the provision of maternal and infant welfare. It forced the recognition in government quarters that the nation was being permanently weakened by the conditions in which so many women and their families were having to live.

Almost more important than any of these achievements was the empowerment and confidence that poor and uneducated women derived from membership of the Guild. For the first time their voices were being heard, and men were being made to listen.

The year after she retired, Margaret was elected President of the Brighton Congress of the Co-operative Union and presented, by both men and women delegates, with an Illuminated Address in which it was said:

> 'For more than 30 years you have been the inspiring genius and moving spirit of this great democracy of working women….. Nor did you make the Women's Co-operative Guild a power only within the Co-operative Movement: you also made it a power in the wider realms of Citizenship…. Above all, the Board value and appreciate all that you have done to shape Co-operative policy in harmony with the Ethical and Moral Principles of Co-operation. As a Teacher, Writer and Leader, you have helped the Co-operative Movement to be loyal to its own ideals and true to the Great Principles which should rule all forms of Human Association. You have never ceased to remind Co-operators of their loyalties and duties as Consumers, Workers, and Citizens, and have shown them how true joy is only to be found in helpful human service. The Board feel that your Presidency of the Brighton Congress comes as a fitting culmination of the work to which they have made reference, and trust that the Co-operative Movement will long have the benefit of the advice and assistance of One whose name will always rank with the names of the Great Apostles and teachers of Co-operation.'

A somewhat fulsome tribute, you might say, but in my view a well deserved one. Members of the Guild were genuinely grieved when she, and at the same time Lilian Harris then Assistant Secretary, retired. One member said:

> 'While we know that there have been splendid workers, we always feel that Miss Davies was 'the Soul' of the Guild, and today at Congress there is that link missing. We miss the personality and that human interest we got from the Secretary and Assistant…..We miss that kindly interest and that little human touch that made you feel as though you were part of the Guild.'

As well as the massive influence she achieved through the Guild, Margaret left two books, which remarkably are still in print. Details of these are in the bibliography at the end of this book. There is a lot of untapped material on her life, for example her long correspondence with Bertrand Russell, now in the Russell Archives at MacMaster University in Canada; her correspondence with her close friends Leonard and Virginia Woolf, which is at Sussex University; and much, much more.

It is a source of amazement to me that no-one has yet written a full biography of such an interesting and influential woman. But I have hopes that this omission will be rectified in the not too distant future.

Later years

For the last twenty years of her life, Margaret became increasingly involved with internationalism and the peace movement and, in particular, cultural relations with Russia. She travelled around the country often staying in small hotels and enjoying meeting people wherever she went. She wrote on one occasion that she had come into 'close friendly contact with seventeen people.' That was perhaps what she loved most in life. I remember well during the war, when she was living with us in the Lakes and physically very limited in what she could do, she would ask to have a chair put outside the front gate so that she could chat to anyone coming up or down the lane. There was no escape for them!

In 1935 Margaret and Lilian, with their doughty housekeeper Mrs Louisa Redhouse, moved from London to Hillspur, a small house next to Burn-twood, Maurice's home on a hill outside Dorking in Surrey. It had been charmingly converted from two cottages by our cousin Janet Pott, who was an architect. Here, as her niece Katharine records:

> 'she was able to surround herself with the graces of art and nature always so important to her happiness; and, even when too old for more active occupations, took delight in watching the birds hop about at the bird table outside her window.'

I remember her room well. It was, as one gathers all her other rooms and homes had been from a young age, beautifully decorated and furnished in the style of William Morris whom she greatly admired. It smelt of pot pourri

or fresh flowers and, as a child, it was always fun to visit her. Living next door, I went often in the months before she died. Before going in, I used to walk past her sitting room French window to see if she was up. So she used to call me her 'Pippa', after Browning's poem 'Pippa Passes.' Sometimes Lilian, whose sight had virtually gone, asked me to read her one or two of Keats' *Odes*, which I grew to love even though I didn't really understand them much at the time, particularly his *'Ode to Psyche'*, which was her favourite. She would hold her ear trumpet near to where I was sitting on the floor so she could hear better. Quite often, I seem to remember, Mrs Redhouse would bring in a cup containing 'Miss Davies's raw

Margaret & Lilian at Hillspur

egg' (always pronounced 'ror-egg'). This frightful cupful Aunt Margaret would gallantly swallow at one gulp. Mrs Redhouse was a devoted and loyal housekeeper. When the local hunt appeared outside the Hillspur gate with the clear intention of riding across the garden, she stood firmly in their way, arms akimbo, saying "Miss Davies does not approve of hunting and you have no right to cross her land."

Margaret died at home on 28 May 1944. After her death Lilian with Mrs. Redhouse moved to Hampton in Middlesex to be near some of Mrs. Redhouse's relations. My mother and aunt, Theo and Mary, used to visit her until her death in her late eighties. Lilian would always have ready a list of matters she would like to discuss with them. The last item on the list would often be 'State of the World.'

The motto of the Women's Co-operative Guild, 'Of Whole Heart Cometh Hope', was inscribed on the silver medallion presented to Margaret in 1922. The inscription on the back, barely decipherable in the photograph, reads:

> 'In appreciation of 32 years service, the Freedom of the Guild is conferred upon Margaret Llewelyn Davies, Portsmouth 1922.'

Of a remarkable family, she was, in my view, the most remarkable member, and the one whose influence was the most widespread and long-lasting.

⑨ Sketch of Arthur

Arthur Llewelyn Davies was born at 18 Blandford Square on 20 February 1863. The third child in the family, we have more information about Arthur than about some of the others because of the events that surrounded his tragic death and that of his wife, Sylvia, three years later. They both died from cancer aged 44, leaving five boys, the youngest seven when Sylvia died and the eldest seventeen. All five were adopted by the playwright J.M.Barrie, who had already played a huge part in their lives and now took over the entire responsibility for their welfare.

The down side, which affected some of them more than others and Peter in particular because of his name, was that they were burdened for ever with being the inspiration for his creation, *Peter Pan*. The story of their lives, loves and the further tragedies that ensued was meticulously researched by Andrew Birkin for a BBC trilogy and written up subsequently in his moving and gripping book *'J.M.Barrie and the Lost Boys'*, published in 1979.

Also surviving are a collection of letters written by Arthur during his first two years at Marlborough, some from his time at Cambridge, and a number on a European tour when he was combining tutoring with sightseeing. Finally there are a few letters written when he knew he was dying. All these letters were selected, edited and annotated by Peter Llewelyn Davies, Arthur's third son.

At Marlborough

Arthur was sent to Marlborough at just under eleven years of age. Charley had already been there for two years and it was another four years before he left. This must have been an enormous help and support to Arthur, although his first letter home gives the impression that he was well able to stand on his own two feet:

> Marlborough, Saturday evening (January 1874)
>
> Dearest Mother,
>
> We got here all right at about a quarter to ten, when I reported to Richardson, and had supper in Hall. I am in C dormitory, the same as

Charles was, and have Eyres, a youth of about 16, for my prefect, not Blackett-Ord. Hunter, a great big fellow, and not very nice, is captain of my dormitory. There are 11 beds in the dormitory, one of which is now vacant, just enough for cricket, and I can't possibly be excluded from the dormitory XI. I was examined this morning by James, a very nice master, and placed in the Middle Fourth A, Voules' form, who (Voules) was asked to play for the Gentlemen v. the Players of England, but refused, as he thought himself not good enough. I like Voules very much. I am going to do select Cicero and Ovid for form work, which I don't think will be difficult, from what I've seen of them. You might think the Cicero would be, but it's select passages of it, remember. In French I am going to do L'enfant des bois, which I don't think is difficult.

The subscriptions are coming round now. I have just paid 6d for Upper School Papers. At the end of this letter I'll give you a list of all the subscriptions. I have just had a mighty spill of ink over desks, form, paper, floor, hands, and a few spots on my bags. All the fellows say how like Charley I am, and some guess my name from that. Today I think almost every boy in the school said to me "What's your name? What form are you in? How old are you?" and at last it became quite worrying to answer all their questions. I always have to say "Daveeeeees." My voice was tried for the choir this afternoon, and I don't think I have got in. Bambridge said "That'll do. Now you can go." He told Norris's brother (who did come to Marlbro') to come to practice this evening, and he's there now. It was awfully light last night coming through the town, ever so much lighter than in London at 6, but it's very dark now. I've bought a cap for half a cr., and I shall get my tin back when I give the tailor an order.

(Sunday) Many thanks for your letter: I got it at breakfast time. I think the jams etc. got here all safe, but I have only opened the potted meat (home-made), the Alberts, and last, not least, the cake, which was awfully good. I like Richardson very much, and A house too. I don't think C's cold's worse. I know I am not the youngest in the school, as when I rep'd myself to Richardson there was another boy in his room, and he asked us both when we'd be 11, and he said he'd be in March. This is a list of my subs.

Rifle Corps 6d. Upper Sch. Pa. 6d . All the rest 4.4 G.T. 5.4

Give my love to everybody. I am your loving son, A. Ll. Davies.

N.B. Please address my letters A.Ll.Davies not Arthur Ll.Davies

Peter Llewelyn Davies comments:

'I can't see how the heart of a mother could desire a more satisfactory letter than this, from an (almost) eleven year old boy writing on his first two days at a Public School. It is happy, high-spirited, full of information, without a hint of any feeling of awe at the new surroundings. It is long; and no longer than many of its successors – he wrote home two or sometimes three times a week. I have nothing to compare it with, but it seems to me that the ease of expression is remarkable in so young a boy.

The handwriting is good without being exceptionally so. There are no spelling mistakes. He uses the long ess when the double ess occurs at the end of a word. It is quite evident that as a boy A.Ll.D was, in the modern psycho-analyst's slang, very much of an extrovert; and also that he and his brothers and sister had been mighty well brought up in the pre-Marlborough stage.'

Arthur at Marlborough

Arthur and Maurice

During his time at Marlborough Arthur, who was already a Foundation Scholar, won both Junior and Senior Scholarships, was a College Prefect and played for the 1st Rugby XV, leaving with a scholarship to Trinity College, Cambridge. His letters home suggest that he was more prone to colds and bad throats than most, and that headaches were a frequent occurrence, not helped, one might guess, by the incredible amount of work he did. However his love of sport and passion for outdoor exercise, which never left him, found plenty of scope in walking, swimming (even in cold weather, it seems) and skating and sliding in the winter and, later, cycling.

The rather splendid posed photograph of Arthur with Maurice, who joined him after two years, shows him to have been of slight build, at any rate compared with his younger brother Hippo, 'the stalwart one'. When that photo was taken at Marlborough, probably in the Autumn of 1876, Arthur would have been thirteen and a half and Maurice just twelve. Until 1878, when Charley left, three of the Llewelyn Davies brothers were at Marlborough together.

Cambridge and after

Arthur got a scholarship to Trinity College, Cambridge, was a Bell scholar while he was there, and left with a first class degree in Classics. Unlike his father and Charley, and later Crompton and Theodore, he didn't achieve a fellowship. He seems to have toyed with the idea of teaching as a career, in spite of having had some rather unpromising experiences helping out at a Sunday School run by undergraduates, which he describes in a letter to his mother:

'I had to hear some little boys a collect, a hymn, and a few verses of the Bible, and didn't particularly enjoy my experience. It is rather disconcerting when one is explaining St. Paul to one child to be interrupted by another with the remark: "Cambridge can't row, teacher", or with an irrelevant question whether I live in College. They also have hateful and elaborate devices for snapping their fingers, and making noises with their fingers in their cheek....'

Arthur in 1890

Perhaps the small pupils, whose interest he failed to kindle, realised that his heart wasn't really in the subject he was attempting to teach.

After touring Europe with a pupil for nine months, visiting France, Italy, Belgium and Germany, Arthur spent a year as a master at Eton before deciding to read for the Bar. He was at the Inner Temple where my mother Theodora Llewelyn Davies, Maurice's younger daughter, would be the first woman to be admitted some thirty years later.

One of the five 'pupils' in his Chambers was Theobald Mathew under whom my mother was a pupil in 1922. She described him as 'the witty and delightful son of Lord Justice Mathew' and recounted how, when she mentioned Arthur, he told her 'his suspicions of his attachment were aroused because he was constantly singing "Who is Sylvia?" in Chambers.' And this was Arthur, who had always disliked sociabilities and had tended to shun the fair sex, leaving Charley to escort Margaret to dances.

Theodora Llewelyn Davies

His hatred of parties was a characteristic he may have inherited from his Davies grandfather, Horace Bach himself, who had once said when some social occasion was in the offing: "Poor as I am, I would give half-a-sovereign rather than go."

His marriage

When he was 26 Arthur fell deeply in love with Sylvia du Maurier. She was the daughter of George du Maurier, who was well known for his cartoons in *Punch,* and would later have success with his three novels, in particular *Trilby.* The two families could scarcely have been more different, the Llewelyn Davieses intellectual and outwardly austere and the du Mauriers bohemian and fun-loving. Fortunately Arthur had the family good looks, felt to be so important by the du Mauriers, as well as outstanding ability and wit, and Sylvia had all the qualities of charm and sweetness that Mary had longed for in a daughter-in-law. They were obviously blissfully happy, even if they were undemonstrative in public, according to Peter Llewelyn Davies.

Arthur's two-year engagement was much longer than those of his brothers because, when they became engaged in 1889, Arthur had yet to make an adequate living as a barrister and there was little money to help on either side of the family.

Photo of Sylvia by J.M.Barrie

On the advice of his uncle Charles Crompton QC, who had always encouraged him and indeed given him some financial help while at Cambridge and later, he joined Maurice then living and working in Liverpool, as it was considered easier to get briefs there than in London.

It is evident that Sylvia was not prepared to make a life with him in Liverpool and we know from Peter Llewelyn Davies's comments that, in the most charming way possible, Sylvia could be very determined. When his Uncle Charles, by this time a widower, died in 1891, he left Arthur and each of the others a legacy of £3.000. He bequeathed the tail end of the lease for his small house in London to Mary, who presented it to Arthur. This enabled the wedding to go ahead. Arthur returned to London and they finally got married in August 1892. Sylvia continued to help the family income, working with the theatrical dressmaker Mrs. Nettleship, who made clothes for Ellen Terry and other well-known actresses. And, by this time, Arthur was showing every sign of becoming a highly successful barrister.

Family life brought fourteen years of great fulfilment and happiness for them both before disaster struck. The births of their five sons, George, Jack, Peter, Michael and Nicolas between 1893 and 1903, were a source of great joy. They moved, after the birth of Nico, to a larger house in Berkhamsted, where the boys could go to a good day school and Arthur commute to London.

Arthur and his sons in 1905

But this happy state of affairs received its first setback with the deaths of two of their parents. Mary died in February 1895 at the age of 61, and then George du Maurier, Sylvia's father, died in 1896, at the age of 60. As in the drawing below, Sylvia had appeared in a number of her father's *Punch*

Sylvia by her father

cartoons. When Mary died, it was a terrible blow to both Arthur and Sylvia. The mother-daughter relationship between Mary and Sylvia had been an extremely warm and loving one. Kirkby Lonsdale never held the same attraction for Sylvia after her death. Many affectionate letters had passed between Sylvia and Mary, whom she called 'my sweet, beautiful Mil' [Mother-in-law]. The following one was written from Kirkby Lonsdale after the birth of Jack, her second son:

My Sylvia, No Mil ever got a dearer or sweeter letter than I did the other day! ... You tell me all so nicely, and I can so well fancy you lying in yr. blue bed, looking so delicious, and yr. two sons with you. Jack seems to make good progress – and never mind if you can't be all in all to him. It is better it should be so for your picking up your strength... Goodbye. I must not tire you, darling. I hope A's cold is better? I shall love to hug you and the 2 sons. Bless you all! M.

The role of Barrie

Sylvia with George & Jack in 1895
Photo by J.M.Barrie

The relationship between Barrie and the five Llewelyn Davies boys, which started when Barrie and his dog Porthos made friends with George and Jack in Kensington Gardens, is now well known.

His devotion in the first place to Sylvia, and later to George and Michael in particular, is well documented. The account, as I have already mentioned, is all beautifully told in Andrew Birkin's book, '*J.M.Barrie and the Lost Boys*', much of it based on Peter Llewelyn Davies's '*Morgue*', parts of which are now accessible on the Internet. Birkin's book covers in harrowing detail the time after Arthur was diagnosed with carcinoma of the jaw until he died, just eleven months later.

It tells of the incredible courage with which both he and Sylvia faced the prospect of his death. The role of Barrie in the whole saga of Arthur and Sylvia's family is a complicated one and we shall never know fully to what extent his obsession with Sylvia and the boys was resented by Arthur. It is clear that Sylvia's devotion to Arthur was in no way lessened by her friendship with Barrie, who was always providing expensive treats and holidays for her and the boys. At the very least his endless presence must have been oppressive at times.

However, even before Arthur's death was inevitable, his career as a barrister became patently impossible through the speech impediment following his initial operation. Barrie's support during those terrible months, and the assurance that he would provide for the family financially, must have eased Arthur's mental anguish in his final weeks, if not his physical suffering.

The deaths of Arthur and Sylvia

Arthur died on 19 April 1907. Sylvia struggled on for three sad years without him and finally died, also from cancer, on 27 April 1910. Seven months before he died, when it seemed that his condition was incurable, Arthur had written to his father:

Egerton House, Berkhamsted, 21 Sept. 1906

Dearest Father,

Whatever may be in store for me, I hope I shall bear it as befits the son of a brave and wise man. I am troubled for myself, but much more for Sylvia. She is brave to a degree that I should hardly have thought possible, busy all day with endless activities and kindnesses for me and for the boys, and all the time the burden is almost heavier than she can bear. Besides her sympathy for me, she shrinks terribly from the loneliness after I am gone. She will have many good friends, but scarcely any one on whom she feels she can really rely. I can see the end to what I may have to endure, but she at present seems to face the prospect of endless misery, and only sees that she must go on for the sake of the boys. I can foresee a not unhappy life for her in the future, with the boys growing up round her, but she cannot now see this. She and all the boys were never so desirable to me as now, and it is hard if I have to leave them. But whatever comes after death, whether anything or nothing, to die and leave them is not like what it would be if I were away from them in life, conscious that I could not see them or talk to them or help them. Barrie's unfailing kindness and tact are a great support to us both....

Your affect. son,

A.Ll.D.

The following letter to his son, Michael, then aged nearly seven, was written four days before Arthur's death. It is his last surviving letter:

Egerton House, Berkhamsted, April 15, 1907

My dearest Michael,

My letters from my boys are indeed a pleasure to me when they arrive in the morning. I hope my boys are getting lots of happiness out of other people's kindness to them and their own kindness to people every day.

It would be fine to have a magic carpet and go first to London, across from Euston to Holborn Viaduct or Victoria, and on to Ramsgate, and see what is going on at Royal (Crescent) and all the other jolly places at Ramsgate. I expect you are having plenty of fun and very fine weather, but that we are getting more flowers, especially primroses. My Nurse is very good at finding primroses and violets.

Your affectionate Father

Of all the letters of condolence sent to family members after Arthur's death that he found, Peter Llewelyn Davies picked out the following one as being 'a singularly beautiful letter – as perfect an example as I ever remember reading of how to do this sort of thing':

Castletop, Burley, Ringwood

23 April 1907

Dear Margaret,

I have been thinking of you all day. So many recollections have been passing through my mind. Do you remember that Charity Ball at which Arthur and Sylvia danced and danced together? I can see your mother's face watching them, and remember her voice saying: "Arthur is rather excited." It was the second time they had ever met. And then I remember going to see them at Abinger when little George was 5 or 6 weeks old. I remember Sylvia bringing him down for my mother and me to see, then handing him over to Arthur, and I can see him kissing the little thing's fingers, as he carried him up the stairs.

The last time we saw him was here, a few years ago, when he brought George for a night on a bicycling expedition. We sat on the lawn where I am writing now. We used to think he was like a young warrior in an Italian picture. And now we know that he was one. The thought of him will be an inspiration to many.

You will not mind my writing, I know, but you will not think I look for you to write.

Ever your affectionate,

Eleanor Clough

Afterwards

The question of how to cope with bringing up the now orphaned boys was difficult. Margaret, already caring for her father and still running the Women's Co-operative Guild, had with great good sense said that she couldn't take on the responsibility, although she had rallied round magnificently looking after the boys during some of the worst weeks of Arthur's illness. I know from my mother that Maurice offered to take two of them, but he was already struggling as a young widower to bring up his own three children. Barrie's wish to adopt all five boys was too good an offer for either family to turn down: any other arrangement would have meant splitting them up

Barrie was immensely wealthy from the success of his plays. So, with the help of Mary Hodgson their devoted nurse, that was the solution. They stayed on in the house in Camden Hill Square that Sylvia had bought after Arthur died. Barrie saw to it that they were brought up in a lavish manner which was a life style that would have been quite alien to their parents and which Margaret, in particular, found very hard to bear.

This is confirmed in an entry in Dolly Ponsonby's diary, dated 7 August 1911:

'Margaret & I talked all morning of Sylvia & Arthur's boys -- & Jimmie Barrie. M. is very desperate at moments about them & I too have felt the pity of their easy, luxurious lives. In fact it has been on my tongue to say to J.M.B. does he want George to be a fashionable gentleman?

Of course in principle he doesn't. In principle he is all for the ragged ragamuffins & says he wants the boys to be for them too. But in his desire to make up to the boys for all they have lost, he gives them every material pleasure. Nothing is denied them in the way of amusement, clothes, toys, etc.

It is very, very disheartening and, when one thinks of Arthur their father, almost unbearable. J.M.B. takes the boys to very grand restaurants in their best evening clothes & they go on to stalls or box at the theatre. They buy socks costing 12/6 a pair & Michael, aged 11 is given very expensive lessons in fly fishing.'

The tragic events continued into subsequent generations. George's death in the 1914 - 1918 war hit them all very badly and Michael's death by drowning while at Oxford more or less destroyed poor Barrie, who had loved him to distraction. Peter committed suicide in 1960. His three sons died prematurely, having inherited the genetic disorder, Huntington's Chorea, from their mother.

10 Sketch of Maurice

Maurice Llewelyn Davies was born at his Crompton grandparents' house at Eardiston in Worcestershire on 13 September 1864. Details of an illustrated account of this eventful family visit, drawn by his grandmother, can be found in the bibliography under the title '*A Victorian Visit*'. Maurice's birth was mentioned by Aunt Emily in a letter to Henry Tomkinson:

Maurice aged 2

> 'My brother is vegetating in Worcestershire. A third little boy is now come to add to our happiness.'

Llewelyn may have been 'vegetating', but certainly his wife wasn't! Named after his father's mentor and hero, F.D.Maurice, he was his parents' fourth child and my grandfather.

But he was more than a grandfather to my sister Mary and me. Our own father, Roy Calvert, had died in 1933 when Mary was nearly three and I was only a few months old. After his death my mother went back to live with her father and sister, so in effect Maurice was a father figure to us, until his death in 1939. I have only a vague but warm memory of him, pushing me in the pram on the local golf course and getting caught in a thunderstorm; reading to us; and, later, of his bed downstairs when he became ill with heart disease. My aunt Mary wrote:

> 'Jane's great predilection for Father goes on – she is always climbing up on him after pushing his paper aside.'

I do remember the smell of his Harris tweed jacket. And I can picture the morning when our mother came and told us that he had died.

Early years

His aunt Emily Davies wrote to Anna Richardson:

> 'I have promised Maurice to report that he, being 4 years old, is 3 feet 2. Perhaps you will kindly measure Phil and let me know his height? Maurice is a good deal <u>thicker</u>. He brought my mother yesterday a kettle holder, which he said was "the third piece of my nice work."'

A few lines written by him when he was four or five have survived:

'Oh! the deep blue sea!
My soul still pants for thee,
In thee the fishes float,
On thee the boat.'

School and Oxford

Maurice followed in the same track as his two elder brothers, first as a day boy at Barfords and then at Marlborough, where he was a Junior Scholar.

In the list of the brothers' scholastic and other achievements, it is noticeable that Maurice did not win a Senior Scholarship nor was he a College Prefect nor, although fanatically keen on cricket and football, did he play in any school team. There is a hint that he was a bit more easy going than either Charley or Arthur and less totally focussed on academic success. When, aged 15, he failed to get a Senior Scholarship in June 1879, he wrote to his mother:

> 'It was Mathematics (of course) and Grammar that settled my chance. I got 100 for Verses and General Paper, 90 for Greek Unseen, 70 for Latin Unseen, 50 for Latin Prose, and 0 for grammar and Mathematics. I do not know what you think I had better do in future. Ultimately I suppose you wish the University.'

On the same occasion Arthur, then 16, wrote home expressing no surprise over the Mathematics but saying that the low Grammar mark was unexpected:

> 'I thought he had done poorly but not so badly as he did. However, as Beesly [A's housemaster] said last night, not getting a scholarship is often really a very good thing; he urged Maurice to work hard now and shew them that he is really the best of the lot.'

It seems this advice was taken and Maurice won a major scholarship to Balliol, choosing Oxford rather than Cambridge because there were no mathematical requirements. This dislike for mathematics seems to have been a long-standing problem. When staying in Oxford to take the entrance scholarship in 1882, he wrote to his father to report on how things were going, mentioning quite casually 'there was a Mathematical paper this afternoon which I did not attend.' A contributory factor to him deciding on Oxford may have been that some of his closest school friends, including Charles Roberts, his future brother-in-law, were going there. In the event the choice turned out to have been a good one as his years at Balliol were happy with many friends and much sociability, and he left with a first class degree in Classics.

But the decision to break with family tradition was a late one, as Arthur was expecting Maurice to join him at Trinity and expressed disappointment over this. He had always taken a close brotherly interest in Maurice, so near him in age. As an example, there is a letter to his mother, written when he was eleven and Maurice just ten, in which Arthur suggests old 'Hippo' should be encouraged to go in for a 'Mnemonics' prize 'as he is likely to get one.' This seemingly involved recitation and also reading a prepared passage, and is an early indication of Maurice's passion for reciting poetry and the ease with which he learned by heart. 'I should recommend him, if he wants to do Milton, to learn the first 300 (lines) of *Comus* .... , as then I could hear him in bed. I advise him, as he likes *Il Penseroso*, to <u>read</u> *L'Allegro*, which I think is the better of the two...' A nice picture of the two young boys, who shared a bedroom at Blandford Square, lying in bed and discussing Milton!

After Oxford

Like his brothers, Maurice did a tutoring job after leaving Oxford. This was a post in Marsala in Sicily, where he stayed for three months with an English family, the husband being the manager of a large wine exporting firm. There were four children and Maurice had the job of teaching the two boys of 12 and 9, who had had little education before, in preparation for school in England. His letters home during that winter give a good account of the simple and uneventful lives of the children and the extreme kindness of the parents. They looked after Maurice in the most hospitable way, though finding it difficult to accept that he was not only a teetotaller and didn't have an enormous appetite but that he also liked to swim in the sea in December and enjoyed a 'cold tub' every morning. The boys and their younger sisters grew very fond of him and he of them. He wrote that, when he left, his were the only dry eyes in the house. But, he added, this might partly be explained by the children having taken an instant dislike to his rather unprepossessing successor who had just arrived.

It was while he was in Sicily that he received a letter from Albert Crompton, one of his mother's brothers, offering him a job in the shipping firm in Liverpool of which he was a Director. Alfred Holt & Co., known as the Blue Funnel Line, ran a fleet of cargo ships mostly to the Far East, and the management were on the look out for some younger people to join the firm. Maurice had been uncertain about what career to pursue and was excited by this offer, only to be dampened by the reaction of his family, in particular his mother. Although we have no copies of letters from his parents or other family members, it is clear from his response that they were all against the idea, feeling the job would not give scope to his intellectual abilities and would be something of a 'come down.' This we can deduce from Maurice's spirited reply, of which the following are a few extracts:

Marsala, 19 Dec. 1887

Dearest Father,

Since getting your letter I have been thinking a great deal about the very kind and unexpected proposal of Uncle Albert and Mr. Holt. The more I consider it, the more clear my feeling becomes that it wd. be a mistake to reject it, tho' I can understand the reasons why you think it would not suit me.

There is on the one hand this very exceptional opening, which it is agreed is ideal if I am to go in for business at all, and which gives me at once regular and permanent work, and I suppose a reasonable and secure remuneration. On the other hand there is the extremely unsatisfactory position in wh. I have stood – with vague ideas of political or journalistic work, but no definite prospect except of hanging about and doing hack work wh. I should detest. I have been longing to get settled and to get regular work.

The family seems to be unanimous in thinking I should require something more intellectual. I think this is a mistake. I have never considered myself essentially 'intellectual' at all, certainly not a born student, and I have never enjoyed study or the exercise of the intellect. It is true I have no knowledge whatever of business but I do not consider myself unpractical. I should not like to feel that I was doing what all the family think to be wrong and foolish. But I must say I think the grounds of objection a trifle fanciful. I do not see anything sordid in the details of business, as far as I know what is involved. There is nothing distasteful to me, at all, in cargoes and crew and captains – rather the reverse. I seem to be regarded as rather a fastidious superfine person who would scorn everything but the transcendental. I feel nothing of the sort myself.

I shall be anxious to hear again – and I much value the family opinion. I hope you will consider what I have said and whether it seems reasonable. Thank Mother for her letter. I shall not like to accept the offer if she continues to dislike it so much.

Your loving son, M.Ll.D

Evidently his parents were swayed by the strength of Maurice's feelings, for his next letter to his mother included the following:

'Uncle Albert asks me to go up to Liverpool as soon as I get to England, and talk things over with him. I am writing to accept and to tell him that I expect to reach England before the end of Feb. I expect the talking over will result in my entering the counting house. My blood will be on my own head – the conscience of the family will be clear: it has warned me of the awfulness of my fate, and I am walking into the pit with my eyes open.'

Work in Liverpool

Maurice started work at Alfred Holt in the Spring of 1888 and remained there all his working life, being appointed a Manager in 1895. Contrary to the dire forebodings of his family, he found the work stimulating and largely enjoyable.

According to my mother, one of his delights was choosing names for the ships, all named after characters drawn from the pages of Homer.

Nestor 1868

Less enjoyable for him, being a poor sailor himself, were the voyages to the Far East and elsewhere, which he was occasionally required to take. We know he was on a trip to Singapore in Ixion in 1894-5, which meant that he was away in the Far East when his mother died unexpectedly in February 1895. This rather poor photo of Ixion shows us the actual ship on which Maurice sailed on that voyage. His mother described it as having a small number of passengers and being 'a new, very fine boat, quicker and carrying a doctor and stewardess.'

The photograph of Maurice in a hat was labelled 'Cairo 1894'. It must have been taken on the voyage out to Singapore.

Ixion 1892

The Blue Funnel line went from strength to strength. Its success was attributed by F.E.Hyde, in his history of the firm from its foundation in 1865, 'to the work and experience of successive generations of men who possessed not only business acumen and outstanding powers of leadership, but were inspired also with a high sense of duty and responsibility.' Maurice was one of these leaders and, when he retired in 1913 at the young age of 49, he was financially secure enough to be able to spend the remaining 25 years of his life comfortably with his family, doing the things he liked to do.

While working in Liverpool and living across the Mersey at Birkenhead, he had time for other interests. His passion for poetry, and the love of mountains that he inherited from his father, drew him to the Lake Poets. As an active member of the Birkenhead Literary and Scientific Society, of which he was for a time President, he delivered their inaugural address on a subject near to his heart: '*Wordsworth After a Hundred Years.*' His statement that he was not intellectual was (to use his own words) 'a trifle fanciful'! Maurice was for many years Chairman of the Girls' Public Day School Trust, which founded many good schools throughout England & Wales.

Marriage

When well established in his job, Maurice received an invitation to be best man at the wedding of his old school friend, Charles Roberts, to Lady Cecilia Howard, daughter of George Howard, the ninth Earl of Carlisle. The wedding was to take place on Tuesday 7 April 1891 at Naworth Castle, home of the Howards, some ten miles east of Carlisle. Maurice travelled there on the Saturday before the wedding and had to leave on the Tuesday afternoon as soon as the festivities were over, to be best man in Yorkshire at his friend Leonard Hobhouse's wedding on the Thursday. During those three days he spent at Naworth, Maurice fell in love with Charles's eldest sister, May. He wrote afterwards:

'My feeling was twofold, one of great enjoyment of her society, she being far the most congenial and sympathetic person I had known, with whom I could converse with a perfect ease and comfort which was a great and novel pleasure; and again, I felt an intense admiration for her character, for the unselfish devotion with which she had taken her mother's place, when only 16 years old, and had brought up, most successfully, a very large family of brothers and sisters, who were all deeply attached to her. In short she seemed to me to combine in a high degree charm and goodness, and so far (tho' in many ways very different) to resemble my dear mother. We made many mutual confidences and our friendship rapidly cemented itself; I felt little doubt she reciprocated my liking for her.'

After the two weddings were over, Maurice returned to Birkenhead and wrote to May proposing marriage. She 'bravely and trustingly replied by return of post, in a short and beautiful letter, accepting my offer and saying that she would try to make me a good wife.'

The reaction to this news at Kirkby Lonsdale was just as warm and affectionate as it had been the year before to Arthur's engagement to Sylvia. There was also an element of surprise as it all happened so quickly. Maurice wrote to Margaret:

43, Bentley Road, Liverpool, Wednesday night, April 1891

Dearest Margaret,

I wrote to Mother last night but as I think you would have left K.L. before my letter arrived I must just send you a line. Wish me joy. I am really actually engaged to May Roberts, C.H.R.'s eldest sister, whom I met for the first time at Naworth ten days ago. Even now I can scarcely realise the fact or all the difference it means to my life. I want not to say much about her till you see her, which I hope will be very soon. I know you'll care about her for my sake first of all & for her own when you know her. She really seems to me the most beautiful character imaginable, -- but you must judge for yourself. I know you will recollect she has lived all her life in an evangelical country vicarage, so you won't expect an intellectual Amazon!

May Roberts

Tell Aunt Carry & Uncle George about it. I know they will sympathise with me in this enormous & sudden happiness that has come upon me. They will soon I hope know and love May. Uncle Albert has been delightfully sympathetic & Philip & Anna very kind. Farewell, dearest sister – we won't love each other the less.

Your, M.Ll.D

According to Peter Llewelyn Davies, Crompton was the most emotional of the brothers. On the evidence of this letter, I would suggest that Maurice was a close runner-up. C.H.R. is Charles Roberts, his friend from school and Oxford; Philip and Anna are Philip Holt, a co-director, and his wife.

Mary wrote at once to Margaret:

K.L.16 April 1891

Well, my Marg – is not this a surprise? I was completely overwhelmed when I read my note last night. Astonishment came first, & then such a joy! One cannot have misgivings when one sees his intensely strong feeling & his tremendous happiness. But is it not wonderful that in 3 days they can both of them be ready to take such a step! 'Love at first sight' is an undoubted fact. No doubt she had known a good deal of him from C.H.R.. How it does change the look of everything connected with him! Liverpool will blossom like the Rose! Dear, dear boy. He will now begin to feel what happiness means – and all that is best & noblest in him will come out.

I feel I can trust his choice – but it is wonderful. Many things he says in his letter are very nice – perhaps he told you much the same – 'When I left Naworth I began to feel the utter impossibility of going on living without her.' 'I have the sweetest, simplest answer.' 'She has been everything to her brothers & sisters. You can't imagine anything more beautiful than it is to see her with them. She seems to me like the sunshine.' ' Recollect she is the simplest possible country girl who has hardly ever been away from home.'

I do long to see her … He wants to bring her here <u>next Tuesday</u> but I urge him not to hurry her. To let her have time to take it all in. She may have misgivings, poor dear, after doing it all so suddenly. But I do long to see her. Shall I once more be watching for the lovers, & seeing them come down the Ch.yard, from yr. window? I gather she is about 26, but he does not say a word about her looks, age or size. How much they will have to discover in each other!

… If only Charley would catch the infection! We see no need to say how short the acquaintance was unless asked. It seems to me that his haste is partly due to all those weary years of doubt and uncertainty he had – he felt it must be done at once. My dear love …

The reference in the last paragraph is to Maurice's two-year, unrequited love for Kitty Lushington, the daughter of a family friend, Judge Lushington. This dream had been dealt a final blow some months before when she announced her engagement to Leo Maxse, Editor of the right wing publication, the *National Review*.

As in the case of Sylvia, May was taken to Kirkby Lonsdale to meet the family. Maurice wrote:

'Few things have given me greater pleasure than to see how instantly charmed they were by her and how fully they approved my choice, which my mother said she was certain I would never regret, as it was based upon admiration of a beautiful and unselfish character.'

Unlike Arthur's situation when he got engaged, Maurice was now securely settled in a job. So they did not have to delay their wedding, which took place on 24 June 1891 at Tidebrook in Sussex, where May's father was the Vicar. This was barely two months after their first meeting and a whole year before Arthur and Sylvia could afford to get married. One could forgive Maurice a little smugness at his own perseverance in accepting the job in Liverpool, overruling his family's advice.

Family happiness and family tragedy

A son, Roland Arthur, arrived in April 1892, followed by Mary in August 1895 and Theodora [my mother] in April 1898. All was joy and happiness until the catastrophic birth of a fourth child in October 1902. Both mother and baby died, leaving Maurice grieving with three children to bring up on his own, then aged 10, 7, and 4.

A few months after May's death, while the memory of her was still fresh in his mind, Maurice wrote a long and very moving letter to his children, which I have, and from which I have already quoted. The envelope is addressed 'For Roland later.'

In it he described in detail how he met May and the immediate impression she made on him. He tried to put in writing how he felt about her, so that the three children would grow up knowing the kind of mother they had had and what a wonderful person she was.

May with Roland and Mary

Poor Maurice. Fortunately he always loved children. According to my mother, when getting a train he would walk along the platform hoping to find a compartment with a 'nice baby' in it. With the help of one of May's sisters, Nellie, who came to live with them until they grew up, and a series of German nursery maids, Maurice managed to keep the family going. He was exceedingly fond of them all three and they of him, and his relationship with Roland was particularly close. The children went to day schools and then to Cambridge, Roland to Trinity and Mary and Theo to Girton.

But it was too good to last. Three weeks before the end of the war, in 1918, Roland was killed in France. The family were devastated. Again Maurice assuaged his anguish by writing what is a touching and interesting account of Roland's too short life. Maurice portrays him as a wonderful companion as well as a very much loved and tender son and brother.

Afterwards

Before this tragedy Maurice had already left Liverpool, having moved in 1913 to Richmond in Surrey. When he had begun to recover from the blow of Roland's death, which seriously affected his health, he turned his attention to encouraging and supporting his daughters in their chosen careers.

Mary was studying medicine and Theodora had decided to be a barrister. Mary, who like so many of that generation never married, stayed with Maurice all his life, as did my mother, apart from the four short years of her marriage. In 1933, after my father Roy's death, Maurice bought Burntwood, a house near Dorking in Surrey, to provide a family home for himself, Mary, Theodora and her two daughters. Before this, in 1920, Maurice had bought

Roland aged 9

a holiday house at Patterdale in the Lake District, near where the family had taken lodgings in August for over 20 years.

Known at the time as 'Place Fell House', Maurice renamed it 'Broad How', which was the older and, in his view, less pretentious name of the small holding on which the house had been built in the 1820s. He saw the forthcoming sale of the house in the personal column of *The Times*, and bought it without having been inside.

This was a highly uncharacteristic action for a careful and frugal man, but he never regretted the purchase. Neither do we, for the house is still in our family. The fact that the poet Wordsworth had once owned the land with a view to building his dream house on the site was perhaps what persuaded Maurice to act so rashly. Wordsworth's signature was on the title deeds.

Broad How in the 1920s

My mother used to say that the purchase of Broad How marked a turning point for him, after a very low period in his life.

Shortly before she died at a great age, our cousin Janet Pott sent me the following description of Maurice as she remembered him on holiday at Patterdale in the 20s:

'I remember Cousin Maurice in his pale blue-green home-spun cloak, which he'd either fling back from his shoulders or, if it was wet and windy, envelop himself in. Of course he knew the names of every peak and tarn that could be seen from every hill top, and he would recite the appropriate lines from Wordsworth, Scott or Coleridge.

In the evenings there would be reading aloud, while the women sewed or knitted or darned. Often it was from 'The Master' – P.G.Wodehouse. There were marvellous refreshing dips into pools in the becks with Mary and Theo (in the nude, which was considered pretty daring then.) Cousin Maurice loved puns and comic verses as well as Wordsworth and I remember his wit and sense of fun.'

Peter Llewelyn Davies recalled a walk up Helvellyn one New Year's Day in the early 20s and

'the satisfaction with which he brought his knowledge of Dryden to bear on a particularly knotty acrostic...He retained his familiarity with the poets...and his encyclopaedic reading must have stood him in good stead with regard to acrostics and crosswords, at both of which he was expert.'

Maurice died at home in Dorking on 19 April 1939. The night before he died a burglar had climbed in at his downstairs bedroom window. Maurice, described by Peter Llewelyn Davies as 'the so-gentle Uncle Maurice', asked the man if he was wanting anything, and the burglar ran away. He died of heart failure the next day at the age of 74, having outlived his five brothers and, mercifully, missing the Second World War by a few months.

With Bridget Fry at Broad How in the late 20s

With Mary and Jane at Patterdale in 1935

11 Sketch of Harry

Harry Llewelyn Davies was born on 7 August 1866 and was the fifth child in the family. Like his brother Maurice he was not born in London but, according to census records, at Markham in Nottinghamshire.

Of Harry as a young boy I have few records and unfortunately no photographs. Throughout his adult life he was spectacularly handsome and shone even in a family where all seven were very good looking. Like his brothers he went to Barfords, where it must have become clear that he was unlikely to get a scholarship to Marlborough as the academic standards there were so high. Haileybury also offered reduced fees for the sons of Church of England clergy, so this is where he went and and he seems to have enjoyed his time there.

In 1881, when at Cambridge, Arthur mentions going down to Haileybury, for a football match:

'I had a good game and a pleasant day, staying there from 11.45 to 9.30. I saw a good deal of little Harry, who was pale, as usual, but cheerful and lively... I saw Butler and Fenning, who gave favourable accounts of Harry. Fenning has a clear idea of his rises and falls in Harry's estimation, and is amused thereby.'

In the summer of 1883, shortly before he left Haileybury, he wrote to his parents that he was in 'intense, extreme, inexpressible bliss'. We don't know the cause of this 'bliss' and of course it might even have been because of his imminent departure from school or perhaps because, as we know, he had been chosen to play for the School Cricket 2nd XI that summer. However there are several other cheerful references to Harry at Haileybury, one being an account of his confirmation and another of his 'glee' when Arthur got a temporary teaching job at the school, standing in for an absent member of staff.

The occasion of Harry's confirmation is recounted in a letter to Theodore then aged 12 from his mother, who was sadly not well enough to go too:

'You can't think what a delightful day Papa had at Haileybury on Thursday. The Confirmation service was very nice and Papa was particularly pleased with the Bishop's (St. Albans) address. The bishop was very friendly with Papa. Harry walked to the station with Papa and there they came on the Bishop again, who conversed with H. and gave him his blessing. And then as the train was just starting H. put his face into Papa's carriage and, on the full grin, said the Bishop had tipped him 10 shillings! That was something was it not? Arthur highly admires the episcopal conduct.'

A number of the mentions of Harry seem to include Arthur who, though the older by three and a half years, seems to have had a special attachment to him, and vice versa.

Living at home

Harry left school just before his seventeenth birthday with the idea of studying at a technical college in London to gain qualifications in engineering. In order to get into the 'Tech' he needed to take an entrance exam in mathematics, so had some extra coaching in algebra. He worked hard and successfully got a place at the college, which was near Bishopsgate in London.

Harry arrived home a few months after Theodore had gone off to Marlborough, thus filling quite a void in his mother's life. She described him as 'a capital companion' and wrote to Theodore:

'You cannot think how fine Harry has made his (Arthur's) room. It is quite a bower of beauty, and he keeps it so tidy and has a duster and dusts it himself! He's a funny boy.'

It is clear from a lot of references in letters to Theodore that this time with Harry on his own was a very enjoyable one for his mother, who was missing 'the little boys', as she called Crompton and Theodore, even when they were grown up. I have very few letters written by Harry himself. The following are extracts from a letter he wrote to Theodore. It gives an impression of the sort of thing he was doing at this time:

Dearest Chubby,

Just a line to say how sorry I am I could not fulfil my long-given promise of sending you a purse before. As you know I had a bad cold before going to Brighton, and Mother would not let me go out of doors… I got it for you today and am sending it off to you. I hope you will like it. I think it is very pretty and has a splendidly strong spring [there speaks the budding engineer!]. I trust it will be of use to you.

I enjoyed myself awfully at Brighton – and have mastered the art of bicycling. It only remains to buy one. I saw some splendid lawn tennis on Saturday …the final draw for the Challenge Cup. I am going to the Lyceum Theatre to see Miss Mary Anderson in "*Ingmar*", with Maurice, as Papa is gone out to dinner and we are left by ourselves. Papa kindly suggested the treat when I wasn't at all expecting it. It was very nice. I have been a good long walk with Maurice this afternoon. Please tell Tottie (Crompton) I am going to write to him again soon.

Ever with much love to him and to yourself,

your very aff. br., Harry.

His time at the 'Tech'

The Tech was something of an ordeal and, for the first time, Harry was working with a much more socially mixed group of young people. His mother wrote:

'He is rather plagued by the riotous behaviour of a few of his fellow students, who shoot paper balls out of catapults during the lessons and sting up the industrious ones. The other day he had a lot of water sent over him and over a just finished drawing, which last was quite spoiled.'

And his father wrote:

'I think Harry is making something of the instructions he receives at the Tech. It would be pleasanter for him if his companions in study were more of his own class, but I believe he does not profess autocratic opinions, but is rather an advocate of equality.'

And there is certainly evidence that Harry was a good mixer and soon made friends with fellow students, who his mother called his 'Technicalities', anyhow enough to play tennis with three of them. It was physically exhausting work, as Mary described it when writing to Theodore in October 1883:

'I can fancy how pale and seedy you would look if you were here in "smoky old London" as Matt. Arnold calls it to the Americans. Harry and Margaret both look such palid (sic) wretches. I am trying to get Papa to take H. for a good airing up at Hampstead this afternoon. He gets very little open air exercise, as he is too hurried in a morning and too tired in an evening to walk to or from his Tech. Coll. He had 5 hours yesterday in the Iron Workshop, hammering, chiselling, cutting at wrought iron, and seemed quite done for when he came home; and could only sink into a chair and listen to his Mith [nickname for 'mother'] read *Adam Bede*. He and Margaret sport a gt deal when he is not too tired, but I think he often longs for his 2 dear members of the chain of love [ie. Crompton and Theodore] ... I'm afraid he'll get quite twintered with all his hard work and want of play.'

And again, the following month:

'You will be glad to hear that our dear Harry, having 3 days holiday – Lord Mayor's Day, Sat. and Sunday – has gone down to spend them at Churt [the home of Uncle Henry Crompton]. I proposed it at breakfast and he was so delighted and off like a shot to catch the earliest train....I hope as the weather is so fine it will quite freshen him up. He gets much less open air and exercise than I approve of in the present regime but is very good and uncomplaining about it. I miss him very much, he is such a dear old sweet Hurl.'

But it was not all drudgery and, from various comments, one gets the impression that Harry entered into everything with enormous enthusiasm. He soon started speaking at the college debating society; the bicycle provided great pleasure; and he went to the theatre whenever he had the opportunity:

'Harry went last night to see Salvini, which has been his ardent desire. The play was '*Macbeth*' and Salvini's first appearance in that part. H. got into the second row of the pit, and he seems to have enjoyed it immensely and to have been greatly struck with the great actor. He took his little red copy and said he could follow nearly every word. I expect he will give us some grand representations of Salvini as Macbeth, don't you? This afternoon the gay youth is gone off to the zoo to see the white elephant. Uncle C. was to have gone with him but was prevented, so he had to go alone, poor boy. How happy he will be when he has some companions again.'

And sometimes the roles were reversed. Margaret had given Harry *The Moonstone,* 'as a prize for being down every day at Prayers for a week! and he says he means to read one chapter a day to me so as to make the pleasure last a long time.'

As well as reading aloud in the evenings, Mary tried doing some French with Harry at this time. She wrote to Theodore:

'H. and I are beginning to read a little French every evening just after dinner. He is very careful and slow in his pronunciation and says I must not throw you in his teeth! But then you have been doing it for so long.'

One can only imagine how galling it must have been for Harry to have all his brothers, and especially the two younger ones, sailing through academic work with such ease. This comment about the French is a small indication of how he must sometimes have felt. My mother told a story that at breakfast, looking through the newspaper and finding a report that an undergraduate had drowned, one of the others said: "Oh, well, Harry will be pleased!" But it wasn't long before Harry's career in engineering took off, and he became expert in an area where none of his siblings could outshine him. Even while he was still at the Tech. Mary described an evening together: 'Harry and I are alone in the drawing room, sitting at the middle table – he working away at his puzzling notes, and I – writing to my small boy.'

In 1885, after two years at the Tech and now aged 19, Harry started work. He went to Glasgow, where he served his apprenticeship in marine engineering with the firm of Robert Napier & Sons, and then worked for some ten years as Engineer on ships of the Bibby line. We have no details of these trips except to know he was on a voyage to Rangoon in the *Shropshire* when his mother died suddenly in February 1895.

Annan

In 1898 Harry started working at Cochran & Co, a general shipbuilding and engineering firm at Birkenhead, where his uncle, Edward Crompton, was a partner of the founder, James Taylor Cochran.

It was Edward Crompton who had designed the revolutionary and soon famous vertical boiler. Amusingly he used the fly-leaf of a

The marine engineer

hymn book for the original sketch during a sermon that was perhaps on the boring side. The year Harry joined the firm, it took the bold step of moving most of its operation from Birkenhead to a large site on the Solway estuary at Newbie near Annan in Dumfriesshire.

Reproduction of an early watercolour of the Cochran works at Annan

This is where, over 100 years later and after many changes in ownership, the firm of Cochran continues to function and where the name of Harry

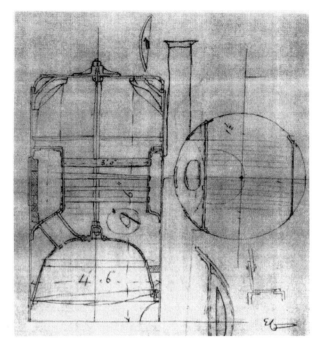

Edward Crompton's original design

Llewelyn Davies is still remembered by some. In 1900 James Taylor Cochran and Edward Crompton retired and Harry became the Managing Director and, from 1904, held the position of Chairman as well, until his early death in 1923. Not long after the move to Annan, the firm gave up the shipbuilding side of its work and concentrated its efforts on producing Cochran Boilers, which rapidly gained a world-wide reputation.

Cochran in 2007

It is interesting that Harry, whose early years may have been more of a struggle and whose academic qualifications were not so impressive, in the end was probably more successful in financial terms than any of his brothers. But, although he became wealthy, Harry was known for living frugally. His egalitarian principles would not allow him to employ a servant, which he could well have afforded, and his beloved Rolls Royce car was an engineer's dream rather than a status symbol.

The Newbie Tradition

Harry played a leading role in setting up the thriving community at Newbie and was in a position to put into practice his passionately held views on equality and social welfare. Together with Edward Crompton's son, Charles Edward Crompton, he set up a Works Industrial Council after the First World War, along the co-operative principles pioneered by Robert Owen at New Lanark in 1800.

These principles had been followed by Sir James Salt in his model village at Saltaire in 1853, by George Cadbury at Bournville in the 1880s, and by others less well known. Margaret may well have advised and encouraged Harry in this, if he needed any encouragement.

The first Works Industrial Council 1919

The ethos once established became known as 'The Newbie Tradition', and the Works Industrial Council flourished for many years. An obituary notice in the *Annandale Observer* of May 4th 1923 gives an account of some of Harry's innovations at Newbie:

'Mr Davies was a keen student of social, economic and political questions. He took a great interest in the social welfare of the employees of the firm, and was the means of establishing societies of a nature calculated to foster the spirit of good will and a sense of the community of interest and ideals among those resident in the industrial settlement at Newbie. He was an ardent advocate of the better technical equipment of the engineer, and for many years he identified himself heartily with the scheme that Messrs. Cochran and Co instituted for giving technical education to the apprentices. Messrs. Cochran and Co were pioneers in providing education for their employees within working hours, and their enlightened attitude was brought to the notice of Parliament by Mr Gulland, then member for the Dumfries Burghs, as an example for general emulation. The classes were ultimately incorporated by the School Board of Annan in the evening continuation system.'

To the Directorate
Messrs. Cochran & Co. Annan
& H.Ll. Davies, Esq.
MANAGING DIRECTOR

Sirs,

The successful termination of the GREAT WAR and the demobilisation of the Army & Navy together with the ratification of the Peace Treaty of Paris have brought in their train many grave industrial problems, much industrial unrest, and the unsettlement of pre-war labour conditions that call for wise & statesman-like consideration & solution, as between Federations of Masters & Workmens Trade Unions & between Employers and Employed. In sympathy with the prevailing unrest, the Employees of Messrs. Cochran & Co., Boiler Works, have made certain claims for shorter hours of labour & higher wages, consonant with the rising ideals for improved labour conditions which the heroism & self sacrifice of the soldiers throughout the War have made it (now that they have returned to civil life) very difficult & indeed impossible to withstand.

With a view to meet in a sympathetic spirit these legitimate aspirations, the Firm has instituted a WORKS INDUSTRIAL COUNCIL wherein the human touch as between Employers & Employed could be the more readily established and, following on the activities & success of this consultative body, the Management has, by instituting A WORKS PICNIC & SPORTS DAY (the first of which was successfully held on Saturday July 12th 1919) impressed upon the Employees & made very apparent the desire of the Directorate to erase doubts or suspicions in the minds of the workmen, the better to establish amicable & friendly relations between Employers & Employed in the Boiler Works.

We therefore, as Employees of the firm of Cochran & Co., do hereby desire to express to Mr. H. Ll. DAVIES, as representing the Employers, our appreciation of these afore mentioned friendly advances, & desire to reciprocate the amicable & friendly spirit in which they have been made. And we further wish to express our grateful appreciation of the very handsome manner in which the Firm has shouldered the financial burden of the Picnic & Sports Day. And we hope that such friendly actions may serve to cement the prevalent feeling of goodwill and be a potent augury of future good relations.

Signed by 27 members of the Industrial Council on behalf of the Employees.

August 1919.

Reproduction of an Illuminated Address presented to Harry in 1919

Harry's political activities

From an early age, along with most of his family, Harry displayed an intense interest in politics. While he was at the Technical College, we read of him attending political meetings and writing political articles and letters, always expressing radical views. As an adult his political involvement is well described in the *Annandale Observer,* in the same obituary notice as the above:

'To a wider public Mr Davies was best known as a politician. He came into prominence when the country was agitated over the question of Tariff Reform and the taxation of land values. He was an uncompromising free trader and on the subject of land values adhered to the group of single taxers. He founded the Newbie Liberal Committee which became a propagandist body of great activity. The Newbie Liberals, while professing general acceptance of the principles of the party, emphasized almost exclusively the vital importance of the two questions which took first place in the mind of their founder and chairman.

Mr Davies himself addressed meetings in all parts of Dumfriesshire, and was certainly the means of introducing a more active element into the political life of the county than that to which it had hitherto been accustomed. Mr Davies was personally popular. He had a fine presence, a sociable disposition and a buoyant and optimistic temperament. As a speaker he had gifts which might have carried him far if he had chosen a public career. He had passion and imagination, and possessed the faculty of arousing in his hearers either unqualified approval or proportionate hostility to his views. As a speaker his style was rhetorical rather than argumentative. He gained a remarkable authority over a public audience both because he understood how to deal with men in the mass, and because he was gifted by nature with the faculties which pre-eminently qualified him to make the best of his knowledge. His management of men was as successful in the workshop and in the industrial council as on the platform, and in individuals he had a power of calling forth examples of personal devotion.'

On another page, the same paper published a graphic account of Harry in action:

'Mr Llewelyn Davies ... distinguished himself as a heckler at political meetings, and on one occasion he caught napping the Unionist candidate for the county, the late Mr J. H. Balfour-Browne, the eminent KC and the then leader of the parliamentary bar. The meeting was at Carruthers Town, and the topic of the hour was tariff reform. Mr Balfour-Browne had devoted his speech to that subject, and as soon as he sat down Mr Davies rose to heckle. He quoted a statement made by the candidate during the evening, and to make sure there was no mistake, asked if that was a correct representation of what was actually stated. 'An excellent and true summary' rejoined Mr Browne. 'How then does the candidate' pursued Mr Davies, 'reconcile that statement with the following extract from a treatise on political economy by an eminent authority?' And, picking up the book, he read out the paragraph to which he had been alluding. 'I cannot reconcile the two statements' at once gaily and confidently replied the candidate, 'they are opposite opinions: but you may take it from me that some of these fellows who write learnedly on political economy don't know very much of what they are talking about.' 'The author of the book from which I have quoted', shouted Mr Davies triumphantly, 'is Mr J.H. Balfour-Browne KC!' The Liberals cheered delightedly, and Mr Browne joined in the general laughter and admitted that Mr Davies had scored. Mr Browne afterwards published a book on humorous incidents at the bar and he included this story among others.'

[It is interesting that the word 'heckler' seems here to mean an active participant at a public meeting without the implication that the person is interrupting and behaving obstreperously, as in modern day usage.]

Marriage and after

It was while he was travelling to Glasgow in the Spring of 1902 that Harry had a life-changing experience. He got into conversation with a young Scottish woman in his compartment. They talked together throughout the journey and shared lunch in the dining car. In the rush of arriving at Glasgow, he realised that she had disappeared without him knowing where she lived. Fortunately he had noticed the name on her luggage label, which was Agnes Macindoe. As soon as he got home he looked up Macindoe in the Glasgow street directory. A great many were listed, so he contacted them one by one and finally managed to track her down.

Harry and Agnes

There was a happy ending. He called round at the house and Agnes herself answered the doorbell. There and then, on the doorstep, he asked her if she would marry him. She said that she would. Agnes was the younger daughter of Frederick Macindoe, a retired stockbroker, and his wife Elizabeth. Harry and Agnes were married shortly afterwards, on 7 August 1902, at the United Free Church of Scotland at Kelvinside in Glasgow. Crompton was a witness at their wedding. At the time of their marriage Harry was 35 and Agnes ten years

'Seven Sisters', Birling Gap, after Harry's death

younger. A daughter, Mary, only survived for a week and they had no further children. They lived at Newbie close to the Cochran works, regularly travelling to the Far East, South America and elsewhere to get contracts for the firm. They also had a bungalow at Birling Gap in Sussex, which they had bought in 1918. It is now the home of my sister Mary, and is pictured here as it was before the war.

Harry died suddenly on 1 May 1923. He had a fatal heart attack while mowing the lawn at Birling Gap. He was only 56 and Agnes outlived him by forty years. The week Harry died, Colonel J.C. Wedgwood MP, a leading figure in the land tax movement, wrote the following tribute for the Dumfries & Galloway Saturday Standard:

'First Theodore and now Harry Llewelyn Davies have gone, those gallant pioneers of land value taxation. I first saw the latter at a small meeting at Clifford's Inn when we were discussing the unemployment of 1905. Then and there I became his follower for life. Perennially young, he was the joy and soul of our movement. Never was he deflected from the unerring pursuit of freedom. For him poverty was caused by unemployment, and unemployment by land monopoly, and nothing else on earth mattered for a moment. He travelled the world for Cochran's Boilers preaching the single tax. He invented children's games to prove the single tax. His

oratory was a torrent of enthusiasm so sincere that it compelled conviction. Such devotion inspires devotion; and all over Great Britain today are little groups of men and women who are feeling as though some of the brightness has gone out from life.'

A wooden bridge across the Milnfield burn on the footpath between Annan and Newbie, taken each day by Cochran workers, was replaced four years later by a stone bridge in his memory. This was a scheme Harry had himself proposed. A bronze plaque was inscribed 'Erected to the memory of Harry Llewelyn Davies by his fellow-workers and friends. May 1927'. The opening ceremony was performed by Agnes. Harry's cousin Charles Edward Crompton, Director of the firm, gave the following tribute:

'Mr Davies was a man of great principles and great ideals. He was almost a visionary. He saw things which could be done which would vastly improve the conditions in which people lived, and he spent much of his time in endeavouring to improve social conditions wherever he went. Newbie might be taken as a very good example of what he was able to achieve in a practical way. His ideal was freedom for everybody, and good fellowship and straight dealing with neighbours. Mr. Davies had left them a happy community and, as far as circumstances would permit, a free community.'

I remember Agnes as an old lady -- she was one of our favourite great aunts. My mother and I stayed with her at Birling Gap the week before I was married in 1955. She must then have been nearly eighty but she still bathed in the sea. This involved climbing down the cliff face by way of a small ladder at the bottom of the garden, wearing a long towelling bathing wrap and shower cap. The following year, after coming to tea with us, she told us, in her delicious Scots accent, that she felt like the small boy who had eaten too much cake. He said to his mother: "Lift me, Mither, but dinnae bend me!"

When Agnes could no longer play the piano, she wrote to the Royal Manchester College of Music and asked if there was a promising student who would benefit from being given her grand piano. They suggested Peter Maxwell Davies, now an internationally famous composer, but then young and unknown. The piano was presented to him and he and Agnes became good friends. Agnes died in 1963.

Harry - study for a bust

12 Sketch of Crompton

Crompton Llewelyn Davies, the sixth child in the family, was born on 13 July 1868 at 18 Blandford Square in Marylebone. Christened with his mother's maiden name, 'Crompton' was usually abbreviated to 'Tony', or 'Scrum' when he was a boy.

I have no material on Crompton as a young child. He followed his elder brothers at Barfords and Marlborough and, like most of them, carried off prizes and scholarships all the way. He also played in the College 1st Rugby XV and was a College Prefect. After winning a major scholarship to Trinity College, Cambridge, in 1887, he was a Bell Scholar and, like his father and Charley before him, was awarded a first class degree in Classics, followed by a fellowship. In 1889 he became a member of the Apostles, the highly select and secret Cambridge discussion society which, as he told his close friend, the philosopher Bertrand Russell, when he in his turn was invited to join three years later, had given him 'a whole

new life' and been 'a revelation of what Cambridge really was.' After leaving Cambridge he travelled in Europe as a tutor for some months and then turned to the law and entered the Civil Service as a qualified solicitor. In 1912 he was appointed Solicitor to the Post Office.

Crompton at Cambridge and after

For most of the material about Crompton as a young man, I am indebted to Bertrand Russell, who devoted several pages of his autobiography to his friendship with Crompton. I quote a few passages:

> 'One of my earliest memories of Crompton is of meeting him in the darkest part of a winding College staircase and his suddenly quoting, without any previous word, the whole of "Tyger, tyger, burning bright". I had never, till that moment, heard of Blake, and the poem affected me so much that I became dizzy and had to lean against the wall. Hardly a day passed without my remembering some incident connected with Crompton – sometimes a joke, sometimes a grimace of disgust at meanness or hypocrisy, most often his warm and generous affection…. He combined wit, passion, wisdom, scorn, gentleness, and integrity, in a degree that I have never known equalled.'

'What made Crompton at the same time so admirable and so delightful, was not his ability, but his strong loves and hates, his fantastic humour, and his rock-like honesty. He was one of the wittiest men that I have ever known, with a great love of mankind combined with a contemptuous hatred for most individual men. He had by no means the ways of a saint. Once, when we were both young, I was walking with him in the country, and we trespassed over a corner of a farmer's land. The farmer came running out after us, shouting and red with fury. Crompton held his hand to his ear, and said with the utmost mildness: "Would you mind speaking a little louder? I'm rather hard of hearing." The farmer was reduced to speechlessness in the endeavour to make more noise than he was already making.'

'He was addicted to extreme shabbiness in his clothes, to such a degree that some of his friends expostulated. This had an unexpected result. When Western Australia attempted by litigation to secede from the Commonwealth of Australia, his law firm was employed, and it was decided that the case should be heard in the King's Robing Room. Crompton was overheard ringing up the King's Chamberlain and saying: "The unsatisfactory state of my trousers has lately been brought to my notice. I understand that the case is to be heard in the King's Robing Room. Perhaps the King has left an old pair of trousers there that might be useful to me?"'

Peter Llewelyn Davies, in his notes on *The Morgue,* picks out Crompton as having been 'the most demonstrably emotional of all the brothers.' The following letter, written to Arthur on the occasion of his engagement to Sylvia du Maurier, illustrates this well:

Kirkby Lonsdale, 6 March 1890

Dear Arthur,

I thought I would not write by the same post as Mother's first letter, but not because I haven't been thinking of you and wishing you all joy. It is indeed altogether joyful, and the thought of you makes everything seem right in the world, everything joyful and delightful. Of course it is only in a dim way that I can sympathise with your happiness, but any one who has ever had feelings of worship called out in any degree, can guess vaguely at the meaning of perfect mutual love. And we know that our gain and joy will not be only that of sympathising with you. We shall owe to you the enriching of our own lives with a treasure wh. I think you may trust we shall know how to value.

We shall try hard to be as worthy of the privilege, knowing well that it is to such as her whom you are bringing among us that we must look for our greatest joy and the strongest influences for all good. Oh, we must try to be nice for her sake. There is no need to tell you how much you and she are in Mother's thoughts, and how Mother longs to see her and make a daughter of her. And there is little need to tell you how the rest of us are entering into your happiness.

Goodbye then till we meet, soon. Your happiness makes us all happy.

In all love, Crompton Ll.D.

Peter continued:

'How such as he could become, as he undoubtedly did become, an exceedingly capable and successful solicitor, and yet retain to the end the same essential tenderness and susceptibility and soft-heartedness, is just one of the many things which go to show that human nature is an inscrutable mystery.'

As the two youngest in the family, Crompton and Theodore did everything together and were devoted to each other. Theodore arrived at Trinity the year after Crompton and they shared rooms, for part of the time over the Great Gate of the College. Both were awarded fellowships in 1894, Theodore, by incredibly hard work, having caught up with his brother.

After Crompton had qualified as a solicitor in 1897 and he and Theodore had passed the Civil Service exams, they both joined Charley in his little house in Barton Street. This was just round the corner from the Houses of Parliament and had at that time many of the attributes of a small village with much sociability, and friends often entertained each other for breakfast. Close neighbours included Adeline and Ralph Vaughan Williams, Mary Sheepshanks and Ernest Shepherd. His mother referred to their household there as 'The Barton brethren.'

The death of Theodore

The death of Theodore in a drowning accident near Kirkby Lonsdale on 25 July 1905, brought an abrupt end to this happy state of affairs. It had a particularly terrible effect on Crompton. This is described by Russell in a letter to Lucy Donnelly on 3 August:

'All other losses seem as nothing compared to Crompton's. They had been always together, they shared everything, and Theodore was as careful of Crompton and as tender with him as any mother could have been.

Crompton bears it all with wonderful courage; his mind endures it, but I doubt whether his body will. I am here to do what I can for him – there is little enough except to sit in silence with him and suffer as he suffers. As soon as he can get away, I am going abroad with him…'

Crompton wrote to Russell at the end of October the same year:

'The loss of Theodore seems still a mere phantasy and the strange mixture of dream and waking thoughts and recollections and fact leave me in bewilderment, but slowly the consequences of a maimed existence remaining for me makes itself felt, as if of a body that has lost its limbs and strength, and has to go on with made-up supports and medical regimen, and resignation to the loss of possibilities of achievement and hopes of sunny days. I cling to you with all my heart and bless you for loving and helping me.'

Crompton and Moya

These 'hopes of sunny days' did however return to Crompton's life when he met and subsequently married Moya O'Connor in 1911, some five years after Theodore's death. They are said to have met at a Liberal party rally, when Moya was working in London in the Civil Service.

Moya O'Connor

She was the daughter of a former Irish Nationalist MP, James O'Connor, who had been imprisoned for nine years for his Fenian activities. She had lost her mother and her four sisters at the age of nine, when they had all been poisoned by eating infected mussels collected by the children from water near a sewage outlet instead of from Dublin Bay as they had been instructed. Moya told how she herself had only just started the fated meal when she misbehaved and was sent to her room. Although she became ill, she was the only one to survive. This terrible episode, of the MP arriving home to find his wife and all but one of his daughters dead or dying, was well known in Ireland, so much so that James Joyce in 'Ulysses' referred to it in the following passage:

'Widower I hate to see. Looks so forlorn. Poor man O'Connor wife and five children poisoned by mussels here. The sewage. Hopeless. Some good matronly woman in a porkpie hat to mother him. Take him in tow, platter face and a large apron. Ladies' grey flannelette bloomers, three shillings a pair, astonishing bargain…'

Whether or not Moya's stepmother answered to James Joyce's description of an ideal new wife for the poor widower, we shall never know. We do know that Moya, who had lived with her father since the family disaster, moved away as soon as he remarried and went to live with an aunt in London.

Many years later, in February 1943, in a letter to a friend, John Cole, Moya wrote:

> 'My early life was anything but sheltered -- most of it was poor, ugly, ignorant and loveless -- the sympathy and affection did not fully come until I met Crompton. Yet the world would not be half so large and rich for me if I had not had those early unpleasant years, and had not mixed with all sorts of queer coves and covesses since.'

Born in 1881, Moya was 13 years younger than Crompton. They were immensely happy together. Peter Llewelyn Davies in his notes said how embarrassed he and his elder brother were as boys by their hand-holding across the table and other 'truly comical' demonstrations of affection between them. Such amorous behaviour was most unlike that of his own parents Arthur and Sylvia who had been, as Arthur himself wrote to Margaret at the time of their engagement: 'at one about outward demonstrations in public.'

The campaign for Irish independence

At the time of their marriage, as Solicitor General to the Post Office and Lloyd George's solicitor, Crompton was a respected establishment figure. It is said that he turned down the offer of a knighthood. This respectability was extremely helpful when Moya became actively involved in the Irish Nationalist movement, since she seemed an improbable spy and, as Crompton's wife, to be above suspicion. Moya and Crompton first met Michael Collins in late 1913, and they both became his close friends and wholeheartedly supported him and the other Nationalists in their struggle

Richard and Seán

for Irish independence. Crompton provided the essential legal advice, briefed Collins on the British delegates during the Treaty negotiations, and actually drafted its terms, although he never took any credit for this. Moya, along with a group of women, played a more hands-on role, smuggling guns and passing on vital messages. Her relationship with Michael Collins was a very close one and there has been endless speculation about whether or not she was his mistress – there seems little doubt that she was. Certainly they loved each other. And I understood from my mother that Moya's views on free love and such matters were 'progressive', at least for that period.

After the 1914 -1918 War, Moya moved back to live in Ireland with the two children of the marriage, Richard born in

Mary Llewelyn Davies

1912 and Katharine in 1915. Katharine was always known in the family as 'Seán' as Richard had hoped for a brother and had given the expected baby a boy's name. This physical separation in no way represented a breakdown in Crompton and Moya's marriage – far from it. My mother told me that they wrote to each other every day and remained devoted. Over the next few years, indeed until his death in August 1922, Moya continued to work closely with Michael Collins and the other Nationalists, taking great risks by providing a 'safe house' in Dublin, as indeed Crompton did in London. In March 1921, owing to what Collins described as an act of gross carelessness on someone's part, Moya was arrested. The Black & Tans ransacked the house but were only able to find a toy gun of Richard's, which they confiscated. My aunt, Mary Llewelyn Davies, Maurice's elder daughter, who was a medical student in London at the time, went over to Dublin to bring Richard and Seán to England. It was thought too risky for Crompton himself to go. Mary, my aunt, described to us the whole adventure and the terrible journey back with the bewildered children, then aged 9 and 6. The crossing was extremely rough and they were all very sea-sick. Mary called up to Richard, who was in the top bunk "Are you all right, Richard?" He replied: "I'm feeling wonderful, Mary – I've just been sick."

Moya spent the next three months in Mountjoy Prison, being released in June and deported to England. Crompton was dismissed from his job with the loss of an annual income of £2,500 – no small sum in those days. His standing as a lawyer was such that he was immediately offered a partnership in a firm of London solicitors. Moya wrote to John Cole, just three months before her death:

> 'Crompton loved his contact with the all and sundry and his contests for his clients, and if there were ever a rich nature it was his. He found the change unpleasant when he became Solicitor to the Post Office -- all humdrum and official -- so that, when he was dismissed (owing to my arrest) though it seemed a bad thing, it was good in the end since it brought him back again to private practice.'

How long it was after her deportation to England in 1921 that Moya and the children returned to Ireland I do not know, nor how much of the time before Crompton's death in 1935 they were able to spend together.

Later years

Russell wrote that, during his last years, Crompton spent much of his leisure time writing a book on philosophy, which had always been 'his main intellectual preoccupation'. When the book was nearly finished he left it on a train, and it was never found. He started all over again, using the few notes he had kept, but it was unfinished when he died of heart failure in the middle of a dinner party in 1935, at the age of 67. My sister Mary, who was five when he died, remembers him visiting at bedtime and his advice: "That's right, Mary. Go to bed with your boots on – saves time in the morning!"

Moya outlived Crompton by eight years, dying of cancer in Ireland in 1943, at the age of 62. Seán came to England and never returned to Ireland, dying in 1995 aged 80 at her home in Edinburgh. There is a short account of both of Crompton and Moya's children, Richard and Seán, in Chapter 16.

Crompton and Theodore as Apostles

13 Sketch of Theodore

Theodore, the youngest of the family, was born on 16 December 1870 at 18 Blandford Square, some ten years after the birth of Charley. While there is always a tendency for those who die young to be remembered with a heightened sense of their brilliance, yet there is plenty of evidence that, in Theodore's case, his outstanding qualities have been in no way exaggerated by his early death at the age of 34.

Early Years

My main source of information about Theodore as a boy is from a collection of letters written to him, mostly by his mother, during his first terms at Marlborough. These have survived by the purest good luck when so many family letters have been lost or destroyed. Sadly there are none of Theodore's letters in return.

Theodore went to Barfords as all his brothers had before him, and took the entrance scholarship to Marlborough in December 1882, a fortnight before his twelfth birthday. His mother, writing to Margaret, described the occasion:

'Theo and I actually start at 9 tomorrow for Paddington for Marl. We chose so early a time that Theo may not be bustled and may get his lunch comfortably before the Nomination exam at 3. I sent Maurice to Ullage [a housemaster] and he found that kind man in act of writing to me to invite, and a most kind note came wh. finally decided me to go. But I wish I felt more up to it. I am very weak and it looks very formidable to poor me who have been shut up so long, with an occasional Bath chair ride for my great last effort.........but, if I can get down there without a 'c'lapse' as Theo says, I think the air and change may do me good. My little darling is in great spirits and excitement. He has a new grey suit and blue tie and a lucky little Billy Cock. He is afraid he shall fail and Papa and I think he may come to grief in his prose as poor Tony did. I told Mr Bell [the Headmaster] that they must not be so distressed if we have to return on Wed. having failed in the preliminary canter! I will send an occasional Post Card. I think poor Papa will feel very anxious for his little beloved one when he is left alone here.'

All apparently went well and Theodore, like his brothers before him, won a Foundation Scholarship. It is not clear when he left Barfords, for he seems to have had a seaside holiday before leaving for Marlborough. On 1 March his mother wrote to Margaret from St. Leonard's in Sussex, describing how, in the coach:

> 'Little Theo was perched up on the box and amused the drivers by chatting all the time. He told one of them he was a Liberal and, he thought, rather a Republican.'

The Marlborough years

The following May, Theodore started at Marlborough where he settled down happily. During his first term both Maurice and Crompton were still there to keep an eye on him. On 8 May his mother wrote: 'I am so happy to think you are so happy'.

On the same day, his father wrote: 'We have been very glad to hear such good accounts, from yourself and your brothers, of your start at Marlborough.'

In June he won a Junior Scholarship, on which occasion Charley wrote to him from Cambridge:

Dear Theodore,

The telegram has just come – excellent news! I am delighted indeed. I expected good news but it is none the less pleasant now that it has come. How pleased they will all be at home. You have the proud satisfaction of earning £60 for the family. You must go on to the £50 next year…

Ever your loving brother, Charles Ll.D.

Theodore went on to win a Senior Scholarship and become a College Prefect, although, unlike some of his brothers, there is no record of any sporting achievements during his time at Marlborough. Of the 37 surviving letters from his parents (mostly from his mother), all written between 1883 and 1884 during Theodore's first two years away at school, I am including one from each parent, although they perhaps throw more light on the characters of the senders than of the young recipient:

5 Blandford Square

24 June 1883

Dearest Theodore,

You will hear about us all from dear and good Scrum [Crompton] who goes back to you today. I tell him I rather envy him to see you and Maurice! but he does not seem to see it. It has been delightful to have him at home, and his eye is so much better that I think there is nothing to prevent him doing work. I hope he will find all well.

A lovely day I am glad to say! Arthur started off on his bicycle after breakfast for Brighton where he is going to stay a couple of nights. He was afraid the roads would be very dirty and heavy, but he will not be plagued with dust.

Then soon after 10 Papa and Margaret (the latter very scrumptious in a white attire) started for the party at (Epping Forest) where they are to meet and lunch with the Waleses and all the Board school children of the metropolis. They are to be back in the afternoon, and then have a wash and start off again for a garden party at the Archb. of Canterbury's at Lambeth. Are they not a gay couple?

As usual I am a victim and not well enough to do anything but lie flat – wh. makes the writing of this rather difficult as the ink will flow the wrong way in the blessed pen. Dear Charley is still here, and we hope to keep him to the end of next week. He is in very good spirits and has been so full of jokes and 'wit' as quite to cut out Arthur this time! He is reading away for his fellowship. Knock at the door and in comes old Scrum laden with Gittens purchases! ....

Oceans of love! Your own dear Mother

We don't approve of yr. eating biscuits.

5 Blandford Square

I March 1884

My dearest Theodore,

We have been wondering whether you and Crompton have escaped colds during this East Wind visitation. It will be very good news if you have. The weather is bracing to those who do not catch cold. We have been very glad to hear of your good places in the Form. And I think you made a very good defence for yourself about your novel-reading. That sort of reading is like a stimulant, which ought to be taken in great moderation.

I think Crompton mentioned the day of the Confirmation, but I omitted to note it, so let him please mention it again. I had a letter this week from 'good Mr. Twit', his godfather. He tells me to my surprise that he is preaching ex tempore in the evenings without a note, and enjoying it. How delightful Sedbergh will be when the Spring is duly come! I wonder where we shall go in the Summer. Your mother seems to think that Chorley is our fate.

I am expecting the *Contemporary Review*, with my article on Mr. Maurice. The '*Life*' seems to be delayed at the printers, and my review will appear before the book.

Good Miss Edith Butler asked me yesterday if I thought it safe to travel by the Underground Railway. I could answer that I thought it specially safe just now, as there is so much extra vigilance. But I do not wonder people shd. be frightened by the atrocities of these wretches. I am quite hoping that the portmanteaus that did not go off will afford a clue for the discovery of the 'miscreants'.

Your most affectionate father

The last paragraph shows that planting explosives on the London Underground is not a modern invention. The account in his mother's letter of Margaret accompanying her father to social events was a common occurrence, since Mary was so often unwell. Hobnobbing with the Prince and Princess of Wales as well as the Archbishop of Canterbury in one day is an indication of the circles in which Llewelyn moved at this time!

Theodore at Cambridge

Theodore joined Crompton at Trinity in October 1888 when he was not quite 17, at the start of Crompton's second year at Cambridge. They shared rooms in the college, at one time, as mentioned in the last chapter, enjoying the splendid set of rooms over the Great Gate of Trinity. Like Charley, Arthur and Crompton (and Maurice at Oxford) he went to university with an Entrance Scholarship. Like Charley and Crompton, and his father earlier, he was a Bell University Scholar and, like all the University 'brethren', he left with a first class degree. In 1894 Theodore was awarded a fellowship for a philosophical dissertation on *'Plato's Theory of Ideas'*. Crompton won a fellowship at the same time, both following the tradition set by their father and Charley.

As was the case with Crompton, though to a slightly lesser degree since Crompton was one of Russell's three closest friends, some of my information on Theodore's time at Cambridge comes from Bertrand Russell's autobiography. There are also various accounts of The Apostles, that secret and highly elite discussion society, of which both Crompton and Theodore were active members. These give glimpses of both brothers as they associated in this august setting with people like the philosopher G.E.Moore, Russell himself, Leonard Woolf, Roger Fry, GM Trevelyan, and other distinguished academics, philosophers and literary figures. The Apostles met every week and one of them read a paper, after which it was discussed and a vote was taken and recorded, though seldom, apparently, on the subject of the original paper! Matters discussed and/or voted on ranged from questions like 'Can God be serious?' and 'Is Happiness a Test of Progress?' to 'Is Indigestion an Ultimate Reality?' and 'Must a Picture be Intelligible?'

At the Treasury

I have found no record of Theodore touring round Europe tutoring, as some of the others had done after leaving university. He took the Civil

Service entrance examination, passing top of his year, and went straight to the Treasury. Here I quote from an article in *The Spectator* of 5 August 1905, reprinted in the Working Men's College Journal shortly after his death. Theodore had been a lecturer at the College for many years:

> 'He impressed his superiors in office, his contemporaries, his subordinates, and Ministers of State who came in contact with him officially, as a man very exceptionally gifted in character and intellect, who was sure to rise to the highest distinction in the service of his country, and to be the life of any cause he determined to support....Young as he was, in the Treasury he was a specialist in questions of local taxation and income tax.'

An example of his powers of persuasion is given by Bertrand Russell:

'He became Private Secretary to a series of Conservative Chancellors of the Exchequer, each of whom in turn he converted to Free Trade at a time when the rest of the government wished them to think otherwise.'

As Assistant Secretary to the Royal Commission on Local Taxation, he drafted the Minority Report, which advocated the taxation of site values.

> 'In the drafting of this Report, in disentangling the rights and interests involved, in helping to find the clearest and most judicious expression for the conclusions of the Committee, his ardour and quick judgment were of the greatest service.
>
> In private life he was always ready with help and sympathy for those who needed it. In talk he was remarkable for humorous and varied comment, and for clear, emphatic statement. In discussion he was a most eager and most courteous disputant. His manner expressed great resolution and the tenderest concern. Many different kinds of men could talk to him on what interested them most.'

His character

Theodore was certainly much loved, not only within his family but among a wide circle of friends. Leonard Woolf described him as:

'a man of extraordinary brilliance and great charm (with a) 'pure chiselled nobility of face, particularly in profile, which perhaps should be called Roman rather than Greek.'

Bertrand Russell called him:

> '...the ablest and one of the best beloved of the family. Theodore and his brother Crompton were able, high-minded and passionate, and shared, on the whole, the same ideals and opinons. Theodore had a somewhat more practical outlook on life than Crompton. He worked incredibly hard and yet always found time to give presents to the children of all his friends, and the presents were always exactly appropriate. He inspired the deepest affection in almost everyone who knew him.'

Russell also wrote:

> 'I never knew but one woman who would not have been delighted to marry Theodore. She of course was the only woman he wished to marry.'

That woman was Meg Booth, the daughter of Charles Booth, the social reformer and founder of the Booth Steamship company in Liverpool. Meg was in love for a time with Crompton, though she refused his offer of marriage a few months after Theodore's death.

'The Benjamin of our house'

When, at the end of July 1905, Theodore's body was found in the Leck beck, where it joins the river Lune near Kirkby Lonsdale, the family and all his friends and colleagues were utterly grief-stricken. Swimming on his own as they often did in one of their favourite pools, known locally as 'Job's Dub', he had evidently, from the deep cut to his head, either slipped on a wet rock or misjudged his dive in some way, and drowned while unconscious. Giving evidence, Arthur told the coroner that Theodore was a strong and experienced swimmer and diver.

Llewelyn, who must have had as his only consolation the fact that Mary had not lived to endure the death of her beloved youngest son, wrote in the Parish magazine:

> 'Readers are aware of the heavy blow that has fallen upon me and my family... A most dear son and brother, peculiarly considerate and tender, the Benjamin of our house, has been taken from us by a sudden, accidental death. Our residence at Kirkby Lonsdale has thus been again associated with a terrible shock and a grievous affliction. It is a mysterious Providence that removes the young from this world and leaves the old surviving.'

Theodore was buried beside his mother near the front door of the vicarage at Kirkby Lonsdale.

Theodore with his father

Llewelyn in front of the vicarage

14 Kirkby Lonsdale

In 1889 John Llewelyn Davies was 'banished' to the small North country parish of Kirkby Lonsdale in Westmorland, where the old Norman church of St Mary's was a Trinity College living. The person least upset by this 'demotion' [as Dolly Ponsonby described it], after his 36 years as the highly distinguished Rector of Christ Church, Marylebone, was Llewelyn himself. He is said to have remarked that he would prefer that people should ask why he was *not* given a bishopric than that they should ask why he *was*. His daughter Margaret wrote: 'Mr. Douglas Freshfield, in speaking of my father on one occasion, said that, though he was not a bishop, yet he had his own cathedral.'

[The German for cathedral is 'Dom', the Swiss mountain which John Llewelyn Davies was the first to conquer. Douglas Freshfield was a well-known British mountaineer.]

The decision not to give him preferment, which lay in the hands of the Prime Minister, Gladstone, can scarcely have come as a surprise, since his overtly liberal views on all sorts of issues had long irritated the mainstream, conservative clergy, as well as Gladstone and Queen Victoria herself, to whom he was an honorary chaplain. It is said that he delivered an outspoken attack on Home Rule in the Queen's presence at Windsor. Perhaps this was the 'last straw.'

On his move from London there were warm tributes from all the organisations and institutions to which he had devoted his energies: from the Working Men's College, of which he had been one of the founders; from Queen's College, Harley Street, where he had been Principal; from the New Hospital for Women, whose Managing Committee he had chaired; and, perhaps most remarkably, 'he received a testimonial to his influence in the shape of a letter signed by some 700 names, including those of nine bishops, 13 deans, many well-known lawyers, doctors, men of science, heads of colleges and schools, professors, and a large body of clergy.' This testimonial was written and the signatures collected by the Dean of Westminster. The following letters were exchanged at the time:

London, February 9th 1889

Dear Mr. Llewelyn Davies,

We, the undersigned, wish to give some expression to our feelings towards you on the occasion of your approaching removal from London, and from the Diocese in which you have laboured for the last thirty-six years. We call to mind your academical distinction, your early ministry at the East End, your labours of more than thirty years as Rector of Christ Church, Marylebone, and as a member of the Vestry and of the Board of Guardians of that Parish, and also as Principal of Queen's College, and as one of the Founders and most constant friends of the Working Men's College. For your wise and unselfish devotion to measures of practical improvement; for the moderation, independence, and charity which you have shown throughout your career; for your maintenance of high ideals, and for your steadiness and judgment in pursuing them; for the influence of your personal character and example, and of your words and writings; for the manner in which you have combined a clear and firm assertion of Christian truth with a generous appreciation of all earnest thought and feeling; and for your habitual sympathy with rich and poor alike, we desire to record our grateful admiration. We should regret your removal less, were it an incident in your promotion to some such high position in the Church as would correspond to your character, experience, and power; but, wherever you may be placed, we trust that your influence may be maintained and increased, and we heartily wish you a prolonged career of usefulness and happiness.

5, Blandford Square. N.W.

February 10th, 1889

My dear Dean of Westminster,

The honour which you communicate to me is one which might well surprise, as well as gratify, a much more important person than the most partial friend can suppose me to be. It implies a singularly generous recognition of what I have aimed at doing rather than have done. I hardly know whether to feel most grateful to the many dear friends whose names I see in the list of signatures or to others whose friendship I cannot claim, who have been good enough to join in an expression of kindness which loving friendship might have prompted.

I may venture to hope that this rare – I might even say unexampled – honour will be of some value in encouraging younger clergymen, by showing them how a humble endeavour to pursue an independent course, and to serve the country as well as the Church in sincerity and hope, has been appreciated by men and women of different schools and parties in the England of our day.

With the deepest gratitude, and with special, special thanks to you, my dear Dean, and to those who with you have promoted this act of sympathy,

I remain, always most truly yours, J.Llewelyn Davies

A further testimonial, with fewer signatories but equally warm-hearted, was presented to Llewelyn by the New Hospital for Women. This was later called the Elizabeth Garrett Anderson Hospital for Women and flourished for over 100 years near Euston Station in London:

To the Rev. J. Llewelyn Davies,

Chairman of the Managing Committee of the New Hospital for Women

Dear Mr. Davies,

As members of the Managing Committee of the New Hospital for Women, we are anxious to express to you our deep regret at the prospect of losing your services as our Chairman owing to your removal from London. You were one of the first, nearly thirty years ago, to encourage and assist the then unpopular movement for the opening of the medical profession to women. Some years later you were one of the founders, first of the Dispensary for Women and Children, and afterwards of the New Hospital for Women, institutions which gave to medical women invaluable experience & which afforded to poor women the option of being attended by qualified practitioners of their own sex. We feel that your never failing sympathy and advice have largely contributed to the success of our work and it has been your encouragement of our plan which has induced us to undertake the building of a new and larger Hospital. In carrying on the work thus begun we shall sorely miss your warm co-operation and wise judgment.

With the renewed expression of our gratitude for much help and kindness, and with the most earnest wishes for your happiness and welfare in your new sphere, we remain,

[Sixteen signatures follow, including that of Elizabeth Garrett Anderson herself, the first woman to qualify as a doctor in this country.]

The Vicarage

The Autumn before the move North, Llewelyn and Mary visited Kirkby Lonsdale to prospect the situation, and have a look at both the church itself and the vicarage, before Llewelyn accepted the new position.

Mary wrote to Margaret on 31 October 1888 in a letter which makes it clear that they had decided to accept the living.

Dearest Marg., Yr. note was a gt. cheer and pleasure this morning. 'All is the reverse of disappointing', dear Papa writes to Harry and Tony, 'except the size of the house.' We both feel that is rather disappointing. It is a small Vicarage, rooms small and not too many. But I think we could make it do, and in some way it is decidedly nice. Bow windows to dining and drawing rooms (one room above the other) at the back, looking over that exquisite view; church more beautiful than I expected. P. seems to be delighted. The

Wares [the current incumbents] very kind and friendly and all parish affairs promising. No difficulty about our not moving for 3 months. The garden (flower) very tiny, but good kitchen garden – field about. Coach house and stables. Town quaint and grey and clean...

'That exquisite view' to which Mary referred was the one immortalised by John Ruskin, and now known as 'Ruskin's View'. Some years earlier the writer and art critic described the Lune valley, as viewed from below the vicarage garden, in 'Fors Clavigera' as:

'one of the loveliest scenes in England—therefore in the world. Whatever moorland, hill, and sweet river, and English forest foliage can be at their best is gathered there; and chiefly seen from the steep bank which falls to the stream side from the upper part of the town itself. There a path leads from the churchyard, out of which Turner made his drawing of the valley, along the brow of the wooded bank, to open downs beyond; a little by-footpath on the right descending steeply through the woods to a spring among the rocks of the shore. I do not know in all my own country – still less in France or Italy – a place more naturally divine, or a more priceless possession of true "Holy Land".'

Mary's description of the vicarage itself as rather small is somewhat surprising. The original building which dates from 1783 was extended in the early 1830's to house a vicar with a very large family. This was done by adding a third storey, which has given the house a rather odd, top-heavy appearance, destroying its classic proportions. The weight of the extra storey was recently found to have weakened the exterior walls and a huge amount of reinforcement had to be carried out in 2006. From the point of view of the Llewelyn Davies family, however, one would have thought the building would have been large enough with only Margaret and Theodore still based at home. In 1889 Theodore was 19 and a student at Cambridge. However one must remember that there will have been several servants in the household.

Anyway, the Red Room on the first floor was allotted to Margaret to use as the headquarters of the Women's Co-operative Guild, and that remained the Guild's national office for the next 19 years.

Life at Kirkby Lonsdale

The little town, described by Mary as 'quaint, grey and clean' was painted in less flattering terms by Margaret's friend, Rosie Nash. In her *Memoir* of Margaret, she wrote of Kirkby Lonsdale:

> 'It was an unattractive little country town, some of the back streets of which were squalid, and its people were of the old, conservative sort, with whom her position as vicar's daughter debarred her from the kind of simple and genuine relation which she would have liked to establish.'

Everything is relative. Margaret, coming from the poor Marylebone parish

where the poverty and overcrowding in the homes she visited as a sanitary inspector would have brought her close to real squalor and misery, might have found Kirkby Lonsdale less depressing than did her loyal friend, sympathising with her on her predicament.

For Mary, who had felt confined in London 'in our old square' and was endlessly pining for country air for herself and the family, especially in the hot summer months, the change must have brought welcome relief and her health seems to have benefitted. She entered into the life of the parish with enthusiasm, ran classes for the town children, did some adult education work, and socialised with other families in the area.

The following letter from Mary to Margaret and Crompton, who were abroad together, was written when they had been at Kirkby Lonsdale for four years. It gives a flavour of Mary's active life at the time and how involved she was with the local community. It also suggests that Margaret had been overdoing things and needed to relax, and that it was Crompton's job to see that she did.

Kirkby Lonsdale

20 October 1893

A few lines of bon voyage to my two beloved travellers! May all go well and happily with you. Get some postcards soon and let us hear just a few words. We are quite in the dark as to yr. route....It's hard to be apart and know nothing of everything. But be sure I don't want you to write much for ever so long. Have a time of do-nothingness, that's my great desire, and I am sure good Scrum will see it's carried out...

A p.c. from Mr Reynolds astounds Papa by hoping to meet him at Revd. Sotheby's wedding <u>next</u> Tuesday! And we had heard not a word of it! Most strange. Poor little man; is he off his head?

I have just been writing to Theo who seems to be flourishing. What a dreadful lot of foreign letters for me to write. I am so busy you can't think – no time to do anything I want. Preps for my two classes take up great time – and plans for the alpine garden – and I've had Miss Fawcett and sister and Mr Whiteside and Miss Wearing to tea, and they all signed.

P. and I have been to call at (the) Grammar School – and at Bargh's farm where they've lost their baby of 14 months. Coming away from there across the fields by Mrs. Roper's, we were followed by an angry sow all the way till we got to Arcum Rd., P. fighting with his umbrella and both throwing stones. It made such a screeching and noise and wd. not be driven.

It was well it was down hill! I was hot enough, and so glad to get through the "squeezer" where Mrs. Pig could not follow. What shd. I have done if alone?

Poor Shap Whiteside had a worse event. Coming home a dark night from High Casterton, by that steep hill, a man sprang out of (the) hedge on him uttering a wild hoop – but little Shap upped with his umbrella and, holding it by the top end, swang the man such a blow that he smashed the numb! I don't know what became of the man – perhaps he lay a corpse on the road.

Now goodnight, sweet and dears. Every good be with you –

Your own M.

As for Llewelyn himself, at an age when most people are thinking of retiring, it must have come as a relief to have left behind many of his highly demanding responsibilities in London and to have moved to a 'lighter sphere of work' in Westmorland. Charley wrote:

'At Kirkby Lonsdale all was as different as possible. There, in the beautiful valley of the Lune, he found a little community of sturdy and thriving North-country people, with practically no pauperism and quite untroubled by "the social problem." The new Vicar became keenly interested in the educational affairs of the parish and county, and took a leading part in the work of the Education Committee of the County Council and of the local grammar school. He used to say that, if people generally had as much good sense and good feeling as the Westmorland folk, there would be no "religious difficulty" in the sphere of education. At Kirkby his Nonconformist parishioners soon learned to esteem and like him.'

To be living among mountains is always a joy for a mountaineer. The fells around Kirkby Lonsdale, so much gentler than the Alps he had loved to climb when he was younger, provided wonderful walking and there were not many days when he didn't go out, either alone or with any of his sons or friends who happened to be staying. Charley described his father as 'an indefatigable pedestrian'. He had always been extremely active and, as a young man, even hyperactive. According to his sister, when Llewelyn was a curate in Whitechapel, his landlady had complained:

'I never saw such a fellow as you, you're always in and out, like a dog at a fair.'

Llewelyn was 63 when he arrived in Kirkby Lonsdale and remained there for 19 years.

The death of Mary

Margaret stayed at Helston in Cornwall for several months over the Christmas of 1894. Letters from her mother make it clear that Margaret was recovering from overwork and stress, and had needed some time on her own, although at various times a friend was staying with her. She wrote to Margaret on 17 December 1894:

Dearest,

I think yr. lodgings sound very good and hopeful; and I hope you will be a renewed creature at the end of them. But oh! How long it does seem to March!...

Mary meanwhile was heavily occupied with a visit of several weeks from Sylvia and her two eldest boys, George and Jack, both of whom were quite ill with colds and coughs. On 6 February she wrote to Margaret, a letter which did not reach her until after Mary's sudden and completely unexpected death from a stroke or heart attack the following day:

Kirkby Lonsdale, February 1895

Such weather I never saw here before. It snowed heavily in the night and all day today with scarcely a break. It is ever so deep – and many degrees of frost. No getting out at all. P. had to bury poor Mrs. Towers in the midst of it all. I saw him well wrapped up. How Miss Redd and my Carlisle girl will get away to their destinations tomorrow I don't know. Miss R. has spent all her days here. It has been too bad for her to go back and forward. What a good thing she is – more of a lady than many so by birth. "You do take such care of me" she said today, when I made her stop her work and sit by the fire with a book till tea – and Kate went in to have a chat with her, being full of sympathy.

Your father is beginning his Oxford sermon on Humility. He is very gay and we are snug together. He is insatiable over the French novel which we find interesting. I fancy the Russell trial is on today and tomorrow. It is to be hoped Arthur will get a good haul from it.

Love to my love, M

The first poor Margaret knew of her mother's collapse and death were the following three rather brutally direct telegrams, sent to her in Cornwall in quick succession on 7 February 1895:

10.30 Prepare to come here. Urgent. Another telegraph shortly. Father, Kirkby.

10.59 Your mother will not recognise you.

1.15 Your mother left us suddenly while dressing.

In a report of her funeral, the local paper described Mary as 'an universal favourite'. This was quite a testimonial since she had only been there as the vicar's wife for six short years. At her funeral the small church was completely full, despite bitterly cold weather, and the congregation included some 400 children from the various schools in the parish.

Mary's death must have hit Llewelyn very hard. They were such a devoted couple and it happened so suddenly, although he must have become used to her periodic illness over many years. Further terrible blows were to come with the death of Maurice's wife May in 1902, the drowning of Theodore in 1905, Arthur's illness and death in 1907, and Sylvia's three years later. For the first time in 1907 there is mention of Llewelyn's own health not being very robust.

So the old man finally decided to retire, at the age of 82. In 1908, Llewelyn and Margaret, with the Women's Co-operative Guild in tow, moved to Hampstead where they lived very near to Emily. He died in 1915 at the age of 90, having been cared for devotedly by Margaret as he gradually lost his independence and, eventually, his eyesight, though not his mental faculties. Emily died five years later, in 1921, at the age of 91.

15　Beliefs & Views

Early influences

Peter Llewelyn Davies observes that the children grew up in a family where they were encouraged to think for themselves, including on matters of religion. Yet the various influences both from their parents and from the extended family were strong and were reflected in the characters of all their children, in the things they believed in, and the way they lived their lives. Llewelyn and Mary between them possessed a rich variety of qualities to which the seven children could aspire; their home provided a fertile environment in which, naturally gifted as they all were, they could and did flourish. There is ample evidence that, when they left the secure and loving confines of the home, they were confident and resilient enough to cope cheerfully with the harsher realities of life outside, from boarding school onwards.

The guidance they received, both by example and precept, was powerful, yet it seems not to have been so oppressive as to give rise to resentment or rebellion. There are plenty of examples in the letters that remain of quite authoritarian attitudes from both parents. Mary imagined that she did not interfere too much with Margaret's life. On 28 May 1892 she wrote: 'Consider what I say. Consider too how little I really interfere'.

However, to the modern parent, some of her advice to her daughter, then a young adult, seems at the very least 'bossy':

> 'Be careful of yourself please and don't do stupid rash things.' (October 1881) and '…you shd. take care. Also, my dear girl, do try and not sit so all bowed together. It made me feel quite uncomfortable to see you, and is merely a lazy trick and most disastrous. I beg you to make an effort in this matter and not to pooh pooh it.' (March 1882.)

More significantly, perhaps, after leaving Girton, when Margaret planned to do some adult education work, giving evening history classes in London, both parents were against it and Llewelyn dug in his heels. Mary wrote:

> 'We have been talking of your proposal and agree it would hardly do. It wd. be much better to try your hand at something rather smaller to begin with. Also Papa says he could not do with your going off to Red Lion Square so late in the evening. "I must draw the line at that" was his remark.'

They all seem to have accepted their mother's endless instructions over health issues, even as adults, and her anxiety in these matters appears to have been carried over to at least some of her children.

There are references to both nervous exhaustion and chronic indigestion being suffered at times by several in the family.

However, their respect for both their parents and for their judgment did not prevent them arguing their case over issues of importance. We saw this in Maurice's spirited determination to go into shipping as a career in spite of their initial disapproval.

Religion

In matters of religion the family were exposed to a variety of views and beliefs. With their father a Christian minister, albeit with unconventional and radical views, one would have expected at least one of his sons to have taken orders, just as both Llewelyn himself and his brother William had followed their father into the Church. This did not happen and indeed, as they grew up, they all in varying degrees veered towards agnosticism and atheism.

At home there were family prayers and the conventions of a Christian household were observed. On Arthur's eleventh birthday, soon after he started at Marlborough, his father wrote:

'I trust all will go well with you, and that you will endeavour to deserve the character of an honourable Christian boy.'

All the children were confirmed into the Anglican Church and there is no sign that they were in the process of losing their religious faith at that stage. It is interesting to speculate on the reasons that may have contributed to this rejection of religion, and when it happened to the different family members. We do know that Arthur and Sylvia had their two oldest children baptised but not the last three who were all born after Mary Llewelyn Davies's death. Maurice and May had none of their children christened. We also know from Peter Llewelyn Davies, who was told so by Barrie, that Harry 'blasphemed, by no means *sotto voce*, at Arthur's funeral, with a thoroughness which scandalised some of the congregation.' Anger at a seemingly needless death is a not uncommon reason for rejecting religion, and some of the family had lived through several tragedies. But this must all remain pure speculation.

Mary's religious views

There is ample evidence in her letters to discount the idea that Mary Llewelyn Davies had no religious belief herself and that it was her influence that took the children away from religion. The rumour, quoted in *The Lost Boys*, that she never attended one of her husband's sermons in all their years of marriage, was not in fact accurate. It does appear to be the case that she found Llewelyn's sermons difficult and so avoided attending them whenever she could. She was 'not keen on meeting Church people who are keen on Papa's theology' (letter to Margaret, May 1889), an indication that she felt unnerved by deep philosophical discussion. This is confirmed in a letter written in July 1888 in which she confided: 'I can't talk on great subjects you know.' And, finally, again in a letter to Margaret in May 1891: 'I never mind what any other preacher chooses to say or think. It's when it's P. it seems to kill me.'

But that she had an underlying belief in some kind of deity and life after death is shown conclusively in a number of extracts taken from her long correspondence with Margaret. She may even have had leanings towards Unitarianism. On 2 May 1883 she wrote:

'I was interested in what you told me of the prayer meeting, and can quite understand your feeling touched by it. Whether it would be a good thing to join in daily I would not feel sure. I think I should be inclined to feel that quiet prayer and thought in your own room and the College morning prayer would in the long run be more wholesome than (what) you describe. I should fear a want of reticence and a too emotional turn when a number of girls together pray in that way. However I have no wish to say a word against anything that could lead to a higher life, which we all must anxiously seek.'

And on 11 June 1883, convalescing at Putney Park after a spell of illness:

'... no doubt there is some purpose in my incapacity – at any rate I like to think so. It may be to teach me patience and submission – and to bring out something in you – if we are unable to do all we could wish.'

At Whitsun 1889, from Kirkby Lonsdale, shortly after their arrival:

'A decorated and full church. The bells began ringing joyful peals before six today. Imagine my joy. I went to early service and found it peaceful.'

And lastly, from Kirkby Lonsdale, she wrote to Margaret just over two weeks before her sudden death:

'(Harry) won't let me be down and fretty – and talks over this and that and everything with me… It was – it must have been – a kind Providence arranged this long stay with me.'

Llewelyn and his Christian Socialism

The influence from their father was very different. Llewelyn had first come under the spell of Frederick Denison Maurice during his final years at Cambridge. 'Spell' is not too strong a word to describe the all-pervasive effect that Maurice had on his followers. Llewelyn wrote: 'Anyone who wished to take a bath in high feelings, let him read Maurice.'

Llewelyn and a group of his contemporaries became disciples of 'The Prophet', as they liked to call him. For Llewelyn, as his son Charles wrote:

'this influence was to mould his whole future life (and), as a theologian, his main endeavour was to spread the ideas of F.D.Maurice, especially in their application to the intellectual and social problems of the day.'

F.D.Maurice, together with Thomas Hughes and Charles Kingsley, had founded Christian Socialism, the Broad Church movement. This combined a belief in the religious principles of Christianity, as propounded by St. Paul, with their practical application in a social context. Thus Maurice and others went on to found The Working Men's College and were active and outspoken proponents for the emancipation of women and education for everyone; and they both led and joined many other radical campaigns.

This hands-on involvement in social issues, so graphically illustrated by Harry's achievements at Annan and Margaret's at the Women's Co-operative Guild, was probably the most tangible effect on members of his family of Llewelyn's Christian Socialism. This was what Llewelyn gave to his children, rather than an inheritance of religious conviction or an interest in theology.

Positivism in the Crompton family

As well as the influence of their parents, the beliefs of the wider family, in particular on the Crompton side, provided plenty of food for thought in the minds of the young Llewelyn Davieses. We know that two of Mary's brothers, Henry and Albert, were leading figures in the Positivist movement, as was Professor Spencer Beesly who married their Aunt Emily Crompton. Positivism, which flourished in the second half of the nineteenth century, and whose name is closely associated with Comte, is not unlike Rationalism or modern day Humanism. It is defined in Chamber's *Dictionary of Beliefs* & *Religions*, as 'any philosophical position which maintains that all genuine knowledge is acquired by science, and denies the validity of metaphysical speculation.' Like Humanism, Positivism had a strong ethical tradition.

As we have seen, the Crompton relations played a notable part in the lives of the family, so Positivist thinking will have been a powerful ingredient in their development. It introduced a strong streak of scepticism into their thinking on religious issues. On matters other than religion, however, it is important to remember that the general tendency towards scepticism that pervaded the family was inherited, at least in part, from their Davies grandfather, 'Horace Bach' himself. The Rev. John Davies, according to his daughter Emily, was apt to say, whenever he heard a good story: "I don't believe a word of it!" Llewelyn too was sceptical, as we saw from Charley's comment when he was eight::

> 'Papa...doesn't believe anything ...he believes in his Church things, but he does not believe that putting stuff on your head will stop you from being bald.'

Political views and allegiance

Going back a generation to Mary's father, Charles Crompton the Judge, one can trace a source of some of the family radicalism. Charles Crompton's electoral manifesto, entitled 'TO THE ELECTORS OF PRESTON', dated

3 September 1832 and sent from York, included the following points later underlined by Harry, plainly indicating his own strong agreement with at least some of his grandfather's views:

'I disclaim entirely the doctrine that the right of suffrage depends upon property.'

'I am opposed to the connection between Church and State.'

'I hate the monstrous monopolies which cramp our trade.'

'I am opposed to sinecures and pensions.'

'I have said, and I say again, and will always say, that one generation has no right to anticipate the resources of a succeeding generation, so as to cause the taxation of the labour of the working classes to an extent which prevents them from earning, by reasonable and moderate industry, the necessaries and comforts of life.'

Mary herself was no less liberal in her views, even if she did have a secret liking for the royal family. Writing to Margaret in 1882 to report that her portrait of 'the dear Queen' had been 'successfully hung this evening', she added: 'Tell it not among the Radicals!' These would seem to have included the entire family with the possible exception of Charley, who is mentioned over one issue as having not agreed with the others politically. The rest of the family were staunch and active Liberals until the Labour party came into being, when those still living transferred their allegiance there.

In 1919, when women had finally got the vote, Margaret walked to the poll in Hampstead, arm in arm with her 88 year old aunt, Emily Davies. Margaret voted Labour and Emily, that great reformer, voted Conservative. Clearly they will have realised that their votes would cancel each other out. But the possibility of not exercising their right to vote, which they and so many others had campaigned so hard to win, would not have occurred to them.

The children's interest in politics began at an early age. As mentioned in Chapter 13, Theodore, when he was eleven, told the coachman that he was a Liberal and 'rather a Republican'; and I don't imagine he discussed politics at a younger age than his older brothers and sister. It is recorded that several of the brothers took part in debates at school and later at University or, in Harry's case, at the Technical College. They regularly attended political meetings and went to hear the great leaders of the day.

A taste of their keenness and involvement is illustrated in the following excerpt from a long letter written by Crompton to Margaret, when she was staying in Rome:

5 Blandford Square

5 April 1887

Dearest little gell, (Margaret was then 26 and Crompton 18)

... I'm so glad you love the dear Italians – certainly when compared with foreigners Englishmen are very vile with their arrogant contempt of all that is not British...

You are missing a very exciting political crisis and some magnificent speeches of Parnell and G.O.M. [Gladstone, widely known as the Grand Old Man]. Parnell literally tore to shreds the Govt.'s case for the Coercion Bill. G.O.M. is very indignant at the Govt. -- the closure against his wishes. Some night soon he is going to make an 'historical' speech on Coercion and Home Rule. There is to be a great demonstration in Hyde Park next (Easter) Monday...

Theo and I are going to get Gerald to come with us. Balfour has been anything but a success as yet; and this bill for destroying Trial by Jury in Ireland for ever, because in one or two counties they have failed to get convictions, and allowing incapable, partisan, ignorant, bloated Anti-National magistrates to imprison any one they like, -- is one of the most iniquitous crimes of the age. Ireland is perfectly quiet now, but if when this bill is passed there are troubles, who can wonder?

Farewell little girl, and great love.

Ever your Crompton.

They were fully prepared to risk witnessing or even getting involved in violent scenes. This is evidenced by the following letter to Margaret in London from her mother, written in May 1887 when she was staying with Maurice in Ramsgate. Maurice was at the time recuperating after some illness:

'In the evening (Maurice) went to an Anti-Coercion meeting because he saw from the papers it had been co-erced, stopped, a few days ago by the base Tories... There was a closely packed room last night, unanimous if provincial, and no need of the stick M. took...'

Harry seems to have been particularly active politically, closely rivalled by Maurice, Crompton and Theodore. But they were all passionate about the issues that concerned them, whether it was land tax, Irish republicanism, poor social conditions, gender equality or, particularly in Margaret's case, internationalism and world peace. They attended notorious trials, such as that of Charles Bradlaugh, who was refused the right to take the oath of allegiance on the grounds that, as an atheist, it would not be binding on him.

Although it seems they were broadly in agreement with each other, there must have been issues on which some of them disagreed. The only mention I can find of such an argument or disagreement (and this may well have involved Charley) is in the following tantalising snippet in a letter from Mary Llewelyn Davies to Judge Lushington, a family friend, and father of Maurice's beloved Kitty, in November 1886:

'Mr Hawkins came ....he wanted to know how the Home Rule schism in the family went on, and whether we had succeeded in "absorbing" the Unionist faction!'

One gets the impression that, on political subjects, there was much open discussion and debate round the family table. Over theological issues, on the other hand, it seems likely that the younger generation kept their dissenting views largely to themselves out of respect and consideration for their father. They were all sufficiently sensitive to realise that Llewelyn's reserve over such matters in all likelihood concealed considerable grief at his children's agnosticism.

16 Afterwards

Heredity is a strange and elusive thing, but some of the genes from Llewelyn and Mary and their children must still live on. I have noticed traits in our own children, and even in our grandchildren, that seem to have come from these particular forebears.

The main purpose of this brief account has been so that those of their descendants who are interested may learn a little about one part of their inheritance. It seemed a good idea to rescue what I could before it was totally forgotten. It has, on the whole, been a fascinating exercise. Considering the patchiness of the material, it is perhaps surprising that the picture that has emerged is as complete as it is, since we have been looking back over some 150 years.

Of Llewelyn and Mary's seven children, only Arthur, Maurice and Crompton had children who grew up. Now, in the early years of the 21st century and three generations further down the line, I can only give a brief account of those of Llewelyn and Mary's grandchildren whom I knew or at least met.

Being in the direct line of descent from Maurice, his branch of the family is naturally the most familiar to me. My mother, his younger daughter, Theodora, had many of the attributes we have seen in her forebears: the pioneering spirit which helped her in her career at the Bar; the dry wit and the use of understatement; the stoicism which saw her through the various tragedies in her own life, her love of literature and her radical views. She never exerted her authority in the home but we trusted her judgment absolutely. She lived until she was 90. Her elder sister, Mary, was one of the kindest and most unselfish people I have known. She left general practice when my father died in order to help with our upbringing. The two sisters made a wonderful team and we three girls were privileged to grow up in such a happy home.

Crompton and Moya had two children: Richard, who had three daughters, and Seán (Katharine) who never married. Richard was an eminent architect who became a Labour life peer and was responsible, with his firm, for the design and planning of Milton Keynes, Euston Station, the Times building, and various hospitals, among other projects. He was a delightful and witty man. His wife, Pat Llewelyn Davies, whom we saw unveiling the plaque to Emily Davies, was also a Labour peer and more politically active than Richard. She became Chief Labour Whip in the House of Lords.

Crompton's daughter Seán was brought up mainly in Ireland and received no formal education, in spite of being academically outstandingly gifted. She was steeped in history and Latin, and had learned some French from a Corsican nun, but was otherwise completely self-educated. After her mother

Moya's death in 1943, she arrived in England and lived with Richard and Pat for some time before making her home with us.

At the instigation of Theo and Mary, who realised her academic potential, she applied for a place at Edinburgh University, to read history. The entrance requirement included a paper in mathematics, a subject for which (like her Uncle Maurice before her) she had no liking, and which she had scarcely studied. So with some coaching she worked to reach the necessary standard. Competition to get into universities immediately after the war was very tough, but a letter of recommendation from a Professor of History at Cambridge secured her a place. A little string-pulling proved to be justified, for she went on to get a first class degree with a gold medal, followed by a Ph.D. She lived the rest of her life in Edinburgh, doing learned research on mediaeval historiographers.

Of Arthur's sons, the only one I myself remember at all was Peter, whose work on the family papers has been such a tremendously helpful resource for this book. He was an immensely tall man, or so he seemed to me, and he came to see us several times during the late forties, when he was working on *The Morgue*. I was in my early teens and we were living in London at the time. Peter's oldest son, Ruthven, was the same age as me, and I remember a wild game of cards at their house with us three girls and Ruthven, George and little Peter. Their tragic inheritance is referred to in Chapter 8.

Of Arthur's other sons who survived and married, Jack and Nico, Jack had a son, Timothy, and a daughter, Sylvia; and Nico had a daughter, Laura. Unfortunately I never met these cousins and can provide no account of them.

I am not pursuing the descendants any further down the years. Suffice it to say that there are plenty of great grandchildren and great great grandchildren, who can look back on Mary and Llewelyn's 'Chain of Love' with affection, if they choose to do so.

Appendix A Llewelyn and Switzerland

All his life Llewelyn loved Switzerland. As a young man he climbed in the Alps and made two first ascents, of the Dom in September 1858, the year before his marriage when he was 32, and the Täschhorn four years later. The full account which follows of his ascent of the Dom appeared in *'Peaks, Passes and Glaciers, a series of excursions by members of the Alpine Club'*, first published in 1859, which led to the birth of *The Alpine Journal* in 1863.

Ascent of the Dom

Till lately, the name and the situation of the highest mountains which Switzerland could call exclusively her own - Mont Blanc being claimed by Savoy, and Monte Rosa, in part at least, by Piedmont - were unknown to ordinary Swiss travellers; and at this moment there are but few who are aware of the pretensions of the peak which forms the subject of this narrative. This obscurity of so high a mountain is partly due to the uncertainty which prevailed till the date of the latest survey, as to which, amongst several summits of nearly equal height, was actually the highest; but still more to the modest and retiring character of the mountain itself, which is almost entirely hidden from the lower valleys by intervening masses, and is scarcely seen from more than one point of view as a distinct and imposing object amongst its magnificent companions.

Those, however, who have had the delight of studying the panorama of mountains from the Gornergrat, will remember that in telling off the peaks from the east northwards, after the Strahl-horn, the Rympfischhorn, the Alleleinhorn, and the Alphubel, they come to two fine sharp summits called the Mischabel horns. These are of very nearly equal height, and both higher than any mountain, except Monte Rosa, which can be seen within the

horizon. The nearer is called the Täschhorn, from the village which lies at its foot, in the St. Nicholas valley; the farther is called the Graben-horn, or, by a pleasanter as well as shorter name, the Dom. On the opposite side the Dom appears to much greater advantage. It is the highest mountain to be seen from the Great Aletsch glacier, or from the Eggischhorn; and one who has been fortunate enough to be on that glacier before sunrise, and to see the fine snowy mass crowned by the peak of the Dom, side by side with the beautiful Weisshorn, receiving the first rays of the morning sun, will remember the sight as one scarcely surpassed amongst the Alps.

The Mischabel horns rise with remarkable steepness between the valleys of St. Nicholas and Saas, the distance from valley to valley at that point, as the crow flies, being only some six or seven miles.

The village of Zermatt, which heads the former valley, being provided with so many more prominent and attractive neighbours, the Mischabel horns have hitherto received most attention at Saas. The curé of that village, the hardy and intelligent M. Imseng, has made several attempts to ascend the Dom from that side; and in 1856, Mr. Chapman also ascended to a considerable height from Saas. I do not know the particulars of these attempts, which may have failed through want of time or unfavourable weather; but probably, even under propitious circumstances, the ascent would be more difficult on that side than it has been found to be on the western side facing Randa. In the summer of 1858, Mr. Cayley attempted the ascent from the latter village, and would, no doubt, have succeeded, had not a mist come on, which stopped him not far from the summit.

Later in the same summer, while spending a few days at Zermatt, I felt the desire to wind up a happy Swiss holiday with some excursion over untrodden ground. Of all mountains not yet climbed the Weisshorn is perhaps the most fascinating, especially to those who have looked at it day after day from the Upper Rhone valley. I proposed, therefore, to Johann zum Taugwald, with whose experience and resources as a guide I was familiar, and whose honest simplicity and quiet good humour make him a very pleasant companion, that we should try to get to the top of the Weisshorn. He thought we might manage it, and we began to speculate on the route to be taken; but, happening to talk about it to Mr. Clemenz, the landlord of the Mont Cervin hotel, I found that he strongly recommended us to substitute the Dom for the Weisshorn. The worthy landlord was also President of the Council of his canton, and took a zealously patriotic view of an ascent of the highest Swiss mountain, assuring me that such an achievement would have " a quite other significance " for the traveller himself, and for the village of Zermatt, than would belong to the ascent of any other mountain. I yielded to his representations, especially as he added that we should be almost certain to reach the top of the Dom, whereas the Weisshorn was thought by many to be inaccessible from the valley of St. Nicholas. My guide was equally ready for the Dom, of which he knew more than any one else, having been with Mr. Chapman on one side of the mountain and with

Mr.Cayley on the other. So we fixed a day; Taugwald engaged a younger Zermatt guide, named Kronig, to act as porter, and on Friday afternoon, September 10th, we walked from Zermatt to Randa, where we were to spend the night.

There is no inn at Randa, but the curé is able and willing to receive travellers into his house, and to give them a bed and village fare. I sat out in the village talking with him, enjoying a delicious evening, and learning something about the educational condition of the country. He had been a teacher for some time at the college at Brieg, a purely ecclesiastical institution, but which imparts a certain kind of knowledge and culture to a good many of the peasants of the valleys. I had been surprised, on an excursion of the previous summer, to hear Johann's brother, Stephan zum Taugwald, say with a smile, as he presented a draught of wine, " Visne bibere, Domine?" and to learn that he spent the greater part of the year at Brieg, preparing to be a priest, and regularly returned to Zermatt for the summer months, to make hay whilst the touristical sun was shining. Many of the priests must be drawn in this way from peasantry of the country; and there may be some who carry studies at the college for a time (the full period being seven years) then withdraw to take to other callings. I made the acquaintance the next morning of a student of this class, belonging to the village of Randa; and as we sat talking that evening the priest exchanged some short remarks in Latin with a neighbour who seemed to be one of the residents of the place. The education of the young in each parish, at least in the remoter and less populous districts, is carried on by the curé, who acts as schoolmaster, and keeps school regularly during the winter season.

I had every inducement to retire early, as there was nothing to do indoors when it had become too chilly to stay out any longer, and I had the prospect of an early call in the morning. There was a great height to climb, apart from any difficulties we might encounter, and I had expected to spend the night somewhere amongst the rocks on the mountain side. But this was voted unnecessary, and we lay down for some broken slumber under the curé's roof. Soon after one o'clock the friendly face of Johann showed itself in my room, and brought a good account of the weather - that anxious subject for all Alpine travellers. We drank our coffee, packed up the day's provisions, looked to the rope and the hatchet, marked the time - ten minutes past two by the curé's clock - and sallied forth by the light of a lantern.

We were soon joined by a volunteer comrade - the student whom I just mentioned - who made up our party to four. It was very dark, and I could see little except the lantern in front of me. But our course from the beginning was a very direct one, varied, that is, chiefly by zig-zags - a style of route by which those who climb steep mountains must be content to have their patience exercised. We passed the first meadows, and took to a path which led through scanty woods to the higher slopes on which cattle grazed, till it grew light enough to leave the lantern behind. Before we left the last trees, the hatchet was put in requisition to provide a small pole to erect as our trophy on the summit, but we were lucky enough to find a substantial branch already cut, which was slung to the back of our Randa volunteer. Then followed a long climbing of rocks, with sometimes a difficult bit giving work to hands and knees, but cheered by the increasing daylight. About the time that we welcomed the first direct rays of the sun, we exchanged our rocks for the short glacier which came down on our right, and then we had a splendid view of the Weisshorn opposite. It was a part of our enjoyment to watch this glorious mass as we rose higher and higher, and its white bosom of snow took so exquisite a tint of soft aerial pink just before the sun shone right upon it, that my taciturn guide, Johann, was himself moved to unwonted enthusiasm. We had everything to put us in good spirits, for the weather was magnificent, the air fresh and serene, the sky without a cloud.

The glacier presented none but ordinary features. We met with something of a wall, which required care and pains to mount; but we were not much troubled with crevasses, and the snow was crisp and not very deep. We made our way towards a rocky ridge which cut into the glacier, where we determined to breakfast.

We stopped here about eight o'clock, to rest and refresh ourselves, and prepare for the stiff part of our day's work. It was already colder than was pleasant, and before we started we buttoned up close, put on gloves, and tied down our wideawakes over our ears. We had not been able to see far above us, and at our breakfasting place, though it commanded a good view, we were not within sight of the actual summit of the mountain. But we knew we had to climb a steep and narrow arête, which stretched upwards on our right in the direction of the peak. The cold wind caught us sharply as we tackled these rocks with feet and hands, and as we stopped now and then to cut steps across a hard slope of snow. But we were soon rewarded by the sight of the Dom, carrying a streamer of powdery snow blowing from its crest.

We had a rather fatiguing pull through deeper snow before we could get to the top. On the side facing Zermatt and Monte Rosa the summit is cut sharply down, and the side at right angles to this, facing Saas, is also precipitous; but in the angle between, facing north-west, the snow lies, though the surface is irregular, and there is considerable choice of precise routes. When you get near the very top, you are obliged to keep close to the Zermatt edge, which resembles the sheer descent from the Finsteraarhorn to the Aar glacier. Such a situation is one of the most impressive to the imagination and to the nerves, but the rope precludes all real danger. So we found ourselves, about eleven o'clock, assembled without any mishap on the actual summit of the Dom.

Unfortunately there is no comfortable seat there. There are no rocks, and though there is plenty of room, the wind blows freely over the snowy platform; so we had to stand in the snow, shivering with the cold, which was sufficiently intense. But what a point for a view we had gained! It seemed ungrateful to think of any drawback to our enjoyment. I had never been at such an elevation before, so it was no wonder that the scene appeared to me grander than anything I had yet looked upon; but Taugwald, who had been very often on the top of Monte Rosa, insisted, with chattering teeth, that our view was greatly superior to that from the higher peak. Certainly it was a point in our favour that we had that beautiful range itself before us. Perhaps, at such a height, the first curiosity is to see how far you can look down. From the edge of our peak, taking care not to trust rashly to the treacherous snow, we could see Zermatt, only a few miles distant, but nearly 10,000 feet below us. It looked very distinct, though minute, and we indulged a hope that some one there might be looking at the Dom, and by the help of a telescope might discern us clustering on the extreme point. We looked down also to the left, upon the broad mass of the Fee glacier, and could easily see the Fee chalets, but Saas and the valley above it for some distance were shut out by some lower range from our view.

But the really interesting characteristic of such a scene as that we had surrounding us, is the host of mountain peaks set in array before you. Those who speak slightingly of the advantages to be gained by ascending to the highest points, do not know what it is to see mountain tops spread out beneath you, almost like the stars of heaven for multitude. The greater ranges rise in mighty curves and backbones, ridged with shining points, and give distinction to the scene; but in that country of Alps, wherever you look there is a field of mountains. The higher you rise, the more magnificent is the panorama you command. And there is no straining of the eyesight here, to pick out some town or natural object which you ought to see but cannot. You give up the plains at once, and the mountains are visible enough. Northwards, we had the Bernese Oberland in full view. The second mountain of that group, the Aletschhorn, which deserves to be climbed for the view it must command, looks well from the south; and is backed by the Jungfrau and its neighbours, with the Finsteraarhorn a little way on the right. Westwards, we have our friend the Weisshorn separated from us by the narrow valley of St. Nicholas. We cannot see Randa, but we scan the whole side of the opposite mountain, and we determine what would be the best route for an ascent. There are fine mountains south of the Weisshorn, but we look over them, and see the Combin standing out boldly, and beyond that the Mont Blanc range, very compact and distinct. Then we come round to the Matterhorn and Monte Rosa, and look over into Italy, where ranges of Apennines bound our view. Eastwards, we have a broad scene of less distinguishable mountains. If I were to fill in the catalogue, however, of which I have given the most important names, I could not impress the scene on the reader's mind. I must be content with protesting that there is a peculiar charm in such a view, which secures every one who ascends a high mountain in fine weather from being disappointed; although, it must be admitted, he may have to set against his pleasure considerable fatigue, and what is more disagreeable, extreme cold. We took some mouthfuls as we stood, but agreed it was no convenient place for a meal. Before leaving the summit we plunged our signpost firmly into the snow, and wrapped a blue apron round the projecting branches, which gave it something of the form of a cross: and, having endeavoured to secure the permanence of this our mark for a few days, we adjusted the rope for our descent.

I cannot at all agree with those travellers who think that any part of a descent is worse than the ascent. It seems to me always easier to come down than to go up; but when you are upon snow the difference is something marvellous. On the Dom, as on the Finsteraarhorn, you can choose, for considerable distances, between rocks and snow ; therefore, if you struggle up on the solid rock, you will be sure to come plunging or sliding down the soft snow. Looking cautiously before us, we descended at a rapid rate, and scarcely paused till we arrived, hot and breathless, at our breakfasting place. There we again rested; and from this point we followed exactly the same path by which we had ascended in the morning. I believe we took each way the best and shortest route, as indeed the time of our excursion would indicate. Our pace quickened as we got gradually nearer to Randa; and when we again entered the curé's parlour his clock was at twenty minutes past four. We had, therefore, been absent fourteen hours and ten minutes.

Of course, we had to give an account of our proceedings to our worthy host and some of the other good folks of Randa. We rested and conversed for about half an hour, and then started for Zermatt, which we reached in time for the evening table d'hôte, to which there was one traveller at least who did justice. I need not say that we were welcomed with kind congratulations. Every community has its own public interests, and a population of guides naturally finds its account in any event which gives it an additional hold upon tourists. I believe Johann zum Taugwald was regarded, in a small way, as a patriotic citizen who had advanced the glory of his commonwealth, and I am sure his own quiet satisfaction was that of a member of his village society rather than of an ambitious individual. I make this remark, because there is a peculiar interest in the simple unartificial socialism, or linking together of private fortunes, which prevails in the Alpine valleys. Sometimes, as at Chamonix, in the guide-system maintained there, the principle is strained till it threatens to break; but generally it does not interfere unreasonably with the convenience of travellers; and for the people themselves it must be very healthy and beneficial. I am sorry to confess that I have no scientific observation to contribute to geology or botany as the result of my day's climbing. It would, however, be rather hard if an unscientific lawyer or parson out on his holiday were to be forbidden to ascend lofty mountains; nor can I quite agree with the censors of such tourists that their ascents may not be useful or interesting to any besides themselves. The particulars which it is in our power to give may be of some service to travellers better instructed than ourselves, and may spread the taste for a pursuit which is as healthful to the heart and mind as it is to the body. The fellow-feeling which animates all who have once become interested in Alpine travel is my excuse and my encouragement for offering the foregoing account of an expedition so deficient in adventure, and so barren of scientific fruit, but proving the accessibility of the elevated centre of one of the finest Alpine panoramas. I have only to add that the height of the Dom, according to Berchtold, is 14,941 English feet above the level of the sea. It may be mentioned, by way of comparison, that the heights of Mont Blanc and Monte Rosa are, respectively, 15,784 and 15,233 English feet. The valley of St. Nicholas, at the bridge of Randa is, by Schlagintweit's measurement, at a height of 4,754 feet, so that the height to be ascended - the village being a little above the bridge - is almost accurately 10,000 English feet.

[Please note that I have not included in the index the many place names that occur in this account, since Llewelyn's ascent of the Dom is somewhat peripheral to the substance of this book. JWW]

Subsequent visits

I have no record of all Llewelyn's visits to Switzerland, but certainly he went regularly and, as he grew older, he would enjoy gentler walking, meeting old friends and collecting Alpine flowers, which in those days was an acceptable pursuit. One memorable visit is recorded in *The Morgue*. In July 1891, Llewelyn and Mary, accompanied by Margaret, Theodore and Sylvia, then engaged to Arthur, visited Zermatt. Llewelyn, who was 65 at the time, wrote to Arthur on 12 July:

> My dearest Arthur,
>
> It is no small satisfaction to find that Sylvia is proving herself so strong and sound and courageous and capable of enjoyment; but it is more delightful to us that a closer acquaintance with her is making us like her better and better, and is strengthening her claims on our affection. No one could be a pleasanter companion; to your mother she makes herself a perpetually charming and helpful daughter. I rejoice that she has come with us on this tour. It has certainly been so far a most prosperous one.
>
> I am astonished at what Margaret and Sylvia can do. After a very severe ascent yesterday, Theodore and Sylvia danced down steep places as if they were just starting. And Margaret has accomplished considerable excursions without being at all the worse. Indeed we all, including your mother, seem to be at our best. But I have made up my mind, without grudging, that I must content myself with efforts suited to my years.
>
> The guide who took me up the mountains thirty years ago is a disabled, but cheerful, veteran with a bad leg. We have both been pleased to see each other.
>
> We are continually hoping that the time of your engagement may not be much prolonged. I have so much confidence in your prospects that I should not be on the side of urging delay. I think we may be able to give you some help for your first year or two.

Your most affectionate father.

Margaret wrote, under this undated photograph of Llewelyn:

> 'Father in Switzerland with his flower tin and glass for drinking from the streams.'

Appendix B Assorted writings

In Memoriam: Theodore Llewelyn Davies

By Augustus Beesly

> Gay laughter, gentle speech; a brain
> To reason's lordship true;
> A soul that flashed back light again
> Like sunshine-smitten dew:
> Ah! Sorrow's self forgets its pain
> In so remembering you.

[Augustus Beasly was a master at Marlborough as well as a published poet. When Arthur's housemaster he became a friend and remained so. His brother Professor Spencer Beasly married Mary's youngest sister, Emily Crompton. Their wedding is described by Charley in Chapter 7.]

In Memoriam: Arthur Llewelyn Davies

By Hugh Macnaghten

> Thanks be to God for all brave men
> And women, and not least for you,
> From show and seeming alien
> To self inalienably true.
> Boy-like you gloried in the strife,
> Wresting from adverse chance, success,
> And love triumphant crowned your life
> And all the rest was nothingness.
> Even in the shadows of the gloom
> You found through all no cause for blame,
> Nor faltered face to face with doom,
> Self-vindicating, still the same.
> And, dying, helpless as you lay,
> Thanks be to God, you helped a friend,
> And kept the single native way,
> With her beside you, till the end.

[Hugh Macnaghten was a Cambridge friend of Arthur's who became a master at Eton. He was the reason for Arthur teaching there for a year before deciding to become a barrister. These are heartfelt lines even if the writer would not have claimed to be a poet.]

Maurice's sonnet to his children

Like one who in a sunny morn of May
Breasted the slope of some steep rugged hill,
Cheered by the song of many a sparkling rill,
With steady step, with spirit elate and gay:
When noon is gone, and clouds obscure the day,
With aching limbs he goes (though resolute still
The day's set task, unfaltering to fulfil):
The skies how dark, how wearisome the way!
So now, with dragging gait my feet I move,
And feel the approach of life's grey afternoon;
Yet will I scorn to stumble and faint so soon,
While Fate still grants what lifts me high above
The pathway's stones and thorns: that precious boon
Which lights the cloudiest hour – my children's love.

[I found this sonnet among family papers. Unfortunately it is undated.]

The following article by Maurice Llewelyn Davies will only be of interest or amusement to people familiar with the Lakeland fells and their names:

Marriage in High Quarters

Our Lakeland correspondent writes:

A wedding of exceptional local interest, the record of which introduces many of the best known names in Cumberland and Westmorland, took place the other day at St. Sunday's, Grey Friars. The ceremony was performed by the Right Rev. the Bishop of Barf D.D., assisted by the Rev. John Bells Banner, B.A., Chapel Stile. The bridegroom was Lieutenant Tom Gill, son of Mr. Stanley Gill, J.P., and grandson of the late General Sir Piers Gill. The bride was Glaramara, daughter of Mr. Stone Arthur Robinson, of Green Gable, High Street, Fairfield, and granddaughter of Dr. Base Brown. Her dress was silk with white side outwards, and green up edge. The scarf gap was filled in with a hanging knot, and the skirt was gathered in crinkle crags, from each of which a graceful bow fell. In her hair was a black comb, and over it fell a costly veil of St. John's lace, originally worn by her great-grandmother, Lady Holme. Her train was carried by a little page, Master Kidsty Pike.

Capt. Harrison Stickle acted as best man, and a guard of honour, drawn from various local forces, attended under Sergeant Man. The bridesmaids were Miss Blencathra Brandreth, Miss Glenderaterra Dale Head, Miss Nan Bield, and little Miss Dolly Waggon Pike. They wore dresses of Mardale Green with grey knots, and for footwear they had chosen the latest pattern of seat sandal. They carried bouquets of old man. An excellent breakfast, which included sundry local delicacies, was served in high style by Mr. Watson's Dodd, and the company did full justice to the cold pike, brown tongue, and hawk's head, nor did the steak pass neglected. Music was contributed by the Lobstone Band, and the well-known peal of 'Cat' bells was rung merrily from the steeple making every pillar rock, by the respected verger, Mr. Aaron Slack, as the happy couple and their attendants left in cars, pursued by the traditional old boot.

A Valentine

Oedipus, not Davies, was the fellow to divine
The name of him I choose to be my faithful Valentine.

My first I safely may pronounce a very useful article;
Of the greatest and the smallest things it always forms a particle.

Of my second I have nought to say, except that 'tis his fate,
Though nobody himself, to help his neighbours to be great.

Though war I hate, yet gladly I join battle with my third,
And shrink not from the combat when the sound of blows is heard.

Now, if my riddles three you solve and in one word combine,
You'll find the beauteous name of him who is my Valentine.

[This is dated February 14th 1877, when Theodore was six years and two months old. His mother must have written it – but did he understand it? For those too young to know, Battledore & Shuttlecock was a popular game.]

Bibliography

Life As We Have Known It by Co-operative Working Women, edited by Margaret Llewelyn Davies, with an introductory letter by Virginia Woolf. These accounts of their lives by several co-operative women were first published by Leonard and Virginia Woolf at the Hogarth Press in 1931. The book was re-published by Virago Ltd. in 1977. ISBN 0 86068 000 2

Maternity – Letters from Working Women, edited by Margaret Llewelyn Davies, was re-published by Virago Ltd. in 1978. This collection of letters , selected by the Women's Co-operative Guild, was first published by G.Bell & Sons Ltd. in 1915. ISBN 0 86068 028 2

Emily Davies and the Liberation of Women by Daphne Bennett was published in 1990 by Andre Deutsch ISBN 0233 9811 941

J.M.Barrie and the Lost Boys by Andrew Birkin was published in 1979 by Constable and Company Ltd. ISBN 0 09 462000 8

A Victorian Visit. This is the story of a visit told in sketches by Lady Caroline Crompton for her grandchildren, Charley and Margaret, edited with narrative and notes by William Wynne Willson. Published by Garland Publications 2007. ISBN 978 0 9558042 1 2

From A Victorian Postbag, letters to the Rev. J.Llewelyn Davies from eminent contemporaries, collected by Charles Llewelyn Davies and first published by Peter Davies Ltd. in 1926. New edition by William Wynne Willson. Re-published by Garland Publications 2007. ISBN 978 0 9558042 2 9

Sources

Much of my material comes from assorted Llewelyn Davies papers and letters, many of which were edited and annotated by Peter Llewelyn Davies in *The Morgue.* The unpublished letters from Mary Llewelyn Davies to her daughter, Margaret, written between 1870 and 1895, are in the archive at Girton College, Cambridge. Other unpublished letters, such as those to Theodore at Marlborough and Maurice's letters home from Sicily, I have in my own possession, and I am also the guardian of Margaret Llewelyn Davies's four commonplace books, compiled by her in old age. Most of the photographs were among my mother's papers. Many of these are studio portraits, others are snapshots from family albums. The portraits of Sylvia were in the leather-bound album put together by Barrie from his own photographs. He presented one copy of this album to my mother, who used to visit him as a young barrister. The reproduction of Edward Crompton's design of the vertical boiler and the illuminated address presented to Harry Llewelyn Davies were supplied by Jim Hawkins and the museum at Annan, as was the photograph of Cochran's first Works Industrial Council.

JWW

Acknowledgements

Copyright permission has been sought for the reproduction of the following photographs:

The print of Christ Church, Marylebone, from Jack Whitehead's *The Growth of St Marylebone & Paddington*, published by himself.

The photographs of Crompton and Theodore as Apostles from *Moore – G.E.Moore and the Cambridge Apostles*, by Paul Levy, published by Papermac.

The line drawing of George Eliot's house in Blandford Square from *Memorable London House*. [I have yet to trace the author.]

The photos of the two ships from F.E.Hyde's book on the history of the Blue Funnel Line and their centenary booklet.

The photo of Llanstinan Church by Ceridwen.

Copyright permission has been sought from the following publishers:

George Allen and Unwin Ltd. for extracts on Crompton and Theodore Llewelyn Davies from *The Autobiography of Bertrand Russell 1872 – 1914*

Chatto & Windus and The Hogarth Press for extracts from *Beginning Again, an autobiography of the years 1911 – 1918* by Leonard Woolf.

I would like to thank the following for their help and/or encouragement:

Andrew Birkin; Ruth Cohen; Annabel Cole; Patricia France; Jim Hawkins, Annan Museum; Ellen Kennedy, Cochran & Co, Newbie; Melissa Llewelyn-Davies; Mary and Michael Mordaunt; Toby Parker, Hon. Archivist at Haileybury; Kate Perry, Girton College Archivist; and Dr. Rogers, Marlborough College Archivist.

I am grateful to my own family for their comments, help and suggestions during the year I have been working on this project; to my daughter, Ruth, for compiling the family trees; and to William, my husband, for much-needed patient technical help and involvement, and for sharing my enthusiasm over what is not, after all, his own family. The cover design, from Richmond's oil painting of Mary Llewelyn Davies, is his.

Index of photographs

Index

[This index covers the main text of the book and does not include references to the two appendices.]

Sussex University 47

Technical College, Bishopsgate 73, 74, 80
Terry, Ellen 54
Tidebrook, Sussex 67
Times Building 114
Tom Brown's Schooldays 24
Tomkinson, Henry 60
Trades Unionism 14
Treasury 36, 95
Trevelyan, G.M. 94
Trilby 54
Trinity College, Cambridge 9, 34, 52, 84, 94, 98
Turner, J.M.W. 102

Ullage, Mr. 91
Ulysses 87
Unitarianism 109
Upcott, Lewis E. 28

Vaughan, David 9
Vaughan Williams 86
Venice 33
Voules, Mr. 51

Wales, Prince of (Llewelyn ap Gruffydd) 7, 13
Wales, Prince & Princess of, 93, 94
Wall, Richard 16
Wares, the Rev. and Mrs. 101
Wearing, Miss 104
Wedgwood, Colonel J.C. 82
Westminster, Dean of 99-100; Abbey 13
Westmorland 45, 46, 98, 104
Whitechapel, St. Mark's 9, 105
Whiteside, Shap 104
Windsor 99
Wodehouse, P.G. 70
Women's Co-operative Guild 38, 43-47, 49, 58, 103, 110
Woolf, Leonard 38, 43, 44, 47, 94, 95, 96
Woolf, Virginia 47
Worcestershire 13, 21, 60
Wordsworth, William 65, 69, 70
Working Men's College 95, 99, 110
Works Industrial Council 78, 79

York 43, 111
Yorkshire 13, 65